DISCOVERING ARCHAEOLOGY

Special Publication

Docent Library

NATURAL HISTORY MUSEUM
OF LOS ANGELES COUNTY

Discovering Archaeology

An Activity Guide for Educators

Shirley J. Schermer

Special Publication
Office of the State Archaeologist
The University of Iowa
Iowa City

1992

DISCOVERING ARCHAEOLOGY:
AN ACTIVITY GUIDE FOR EDUCATORS

by Shirley J. Schermer

A special publication of the
Office of the State Archaeologist
The University of Iowa
Iowa City

Published with the assistance of the
Iowa Conservation Education Council

Stephen C. Lensink and
Julianne L. Hoyer, Editors

William Green, State Archaeologist

Library of Congress Cataloging-in-Publication Data

Schermer, Shirley J.
    Discovering Archaeology: An Activity Guide for Educators / Shirley J. Schermer
    p.   cm. — (A special publication of the Office of the State Archaeologist)
Includes bibliographical references.
ISBN 0-87414-087-0
    1. Archaeology—Study and teaching. I. Title. II. Series: Special publication (Iowa. Office of
State Archaeologist)
CC83.S34   1992
930.1'07 2' —dc20

Table of Contents

Page

Acknowledgments   vii

What is Archaeology?   1

Evidence for the Past   3

    Activity 1. What is an Artifact?   4

    Activity 2. Symbolic Versus Practical Objects   6

The Work of Archaeologists   8

    Activity 3. Picnic Ground Archaeology   11

    Activity 4. Garbage Can Archaeology   13

    Activity 5. Simulated Dig   15

Pottery   17

    Activity 6. Pottery Making   18

Prehistoric Use of Natural Resources for Tools, Shelter, and Food   20

    Activity 7. Resources for Tools and Shelter   22

    Activity 8. Resources for Food   24

Birds in Prehistory   26

    Activity 9. Bird Identification   28

Archaeological Ethics and Law   30

    Activity 10. Archaeology and You   34

Glossary   36

References   37

Appendix A. A Brief Culture History of Iowa (by Shirley J. Schermer,
    William Green, and James M. Collins)   42

Appendix B. A Selected List of Archaeological Sites, Museums, and
    Resource Centers in Iowa   48

Appendix C. Bone Tools (by Toby Morrow)   50

Illustration Credits   54

Iowa Archeological Society Application Form   55

Acknowledgments

The idea for this activity guide originated with Sharon Kaufman, naturalist with the Des Moines County Conservation Board. Her ideas and enthusiasm along with those of Deb Zieglowsky Baker and the support of the Iowa Conservation Education Council were instrumental in launching this project. Deb Zieglowsky Baker, Mark Anderson, John Cordell, and Dan Mascal provided valuable input in the development of the various activities. Gail Wortmann graciously granted permission to adapt her activity "An Archaeological Dig" for use in this guide. Toby Morrow provided permission to use his manual on bone tools for inclusion as Appendix C. Portions of the text were adapted from the Office of the State Archaeologist's P.A.S.T. and Educational Series materials. Acknowledgment is given to Lynn Marie Alex, Julianne Hoyer, and Duane Anderson for their earlier efforts with producing those materials.

The Iowa Humanities Board provided a grant to conduct workshops to introduce a draft version of the guide to naturalists and educators, field test the activities, and get feedback before the guide was finalized. Special thanks go to Sharon Kaufman, Dawn Snyder, and Ann Burns for organizing the workshops, field testing the activities, and providing comments on the draft copy of the guide. Thanks also go to Joe Artz, Douglas Schermer, and Robin Lillie for comments and suggestions, and to Linda Langenberg for her word-processing expertise.

What Is Archaeology?

The field of archaeology is not always accurately understood by the general public. The archaeologist is often popularly portrayed as a treasure hunter—like an "Indiana Jones"—with a career full of excitement and incredible adventures. In reality, much of what archaeologists do, indeed, what all scientists do, might be considered by many to be tedious and boring. People also often confuse archaeology with other disciplines such as **geology**—the study of the earth and the rocks of which it is composed—and **paleontology**—the study of plant and animal fossil remains.

So what is archaeology? Archaeology as a discipline is a subfield of anthropology. It is the study of the material remains of past human behavior within specific historic and ecological frameworks. Material objects refer to such things as tools, clothing, houses, food, and means of transportation. Cultural behavior also includes the nonmaterial—social organization, language, and beliefs. A key concept in understanding culture is that there are *patterns* of behavior and ideas. By examining the patterning of material objects, archaeologists try to interpret the behavior that produced the objects.

Culture can be thought of as a system of interacting elements where a change in one aspect of the system may cause changes in other aspects. These elements include subsistence economy (food procurement), technology, social organization, ideology (beliefs and religion), and language.

There is also an interaction between culture and the environment. Culture is the uniquely human way of adapting to both the physical and social environment. Archaeology attempts to reconstruct past lifeways and also studies the cultural processes involved in these lifeways. Archaeologists want to understand how and why human cultures have changed in the past. They then try to share their interpretations with the public.

There are several types of archaeology—prehistoric, historical, classical, and underwater. The first two will be discussed briefly. **Prehistoric archaeologists** study human prehistory, the period before written history. With no written documents available, the material remains left by these past cultures are the primary evidence archaeologists have to reconstruct the past. Prehistory is the overwhelming portion of the total human story. The human species had its beginnings at least five million years ago. Modern humans, *Homo sapiens sapiens,* appeared approximately 40,000 years ago. The first writing appeared in Mesopotamia only 5,500 years ago. Although pictographic devices called "codices" and "winter counts" were used as mnemonic devices, there were no written records north of Mexico until the early European explorers arrived.

Historical archaeologists study cultures for which there are written records. Although they share techniques and methodology with prehistoric archaeologists, historical archaeologists have the advantage of the availability of written records that can help guide their research as well as supplement the archaeological data. The archaeological data can, in turn, supplement the written records. While historical accounts focus on describing or explaining sequences of events or important historical individuals, historical archaeology can play an important role in providing a more complete picture of the historic past. It can provide important information on daily life which is lacking in documents alone. Reconstructions of early settlements and interpretations of life there have been greatly assisted by archaeological research at historic sites such as Plymouth Colony, Jamestown, and Colonial Williamsburg.

In archaeology, we use fragmentary data upon which to reconstruct the past. All cultural material remains are perishable, but some are more perishable than others. A tomato peel left at a site will soon disappear by organic decomposition; a stone ax will last millions of years. Archaeologists generally find only the less perishable artifacts and remains. It has been estimated that

90–99 percent of all material objects left behind when people abandon a site are lost forever through decomposition and decay. Bits of pottery, broken bones, and stone tools cannot provide us with enough evidence to reconstruct a total picture of a cultural system any more than the contents of your trash barrel reflect the totality of modern American society.

Yet, to a certain extent, aspects of nonmaterial culture can be reconstructed from such data. Inferences about a culture's technology and subsistence economy can more confidently be made than about their ideology or social organization. However, even these less tangible aspects of a culture are reflected in the artifacts of a people. In our own society, for instance, religious beliefs are expressed in objects such as crosses, statuary, and painting as well as in churches and synagogues. The archaeologist of the future, lacking written records, would be able to infer something of our religious beliefs by studying the patterns of these material remains and their associations.

Information about social organization is provided in a number of ways. The size of our towns and cities, the number of buildings such as houses, stores, or schools, and their proximity to one another indicate the size of our communities. The different types of buildings and the items they contain point to various functions of our structures. An archaeologist would have little difficulty telling the difference between a factory and a house based on the size of these structures, the layout of the rooms, and the contents of each.

In the following activities, we hope students will come to understand how the archaeologist interprets evidence to make inferences about prehistoric life. We also hope the students will develop a deeper awareness and understanding of the interaction between humans and their physical environment.

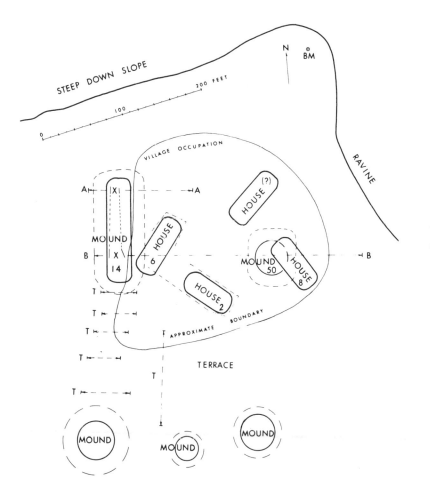

An archaeologist's map of a prehistoric Indian village in northeastern Iowa.

Evidence for the Past

Where do archaeological data originate? As a scientist, the archaeologist attempts to derive explanations about culture through observation and description. Unlike chemists or physicists whose experiments are conducted in the laboratory, archaeologists must make their observations in the field through the study of archaeological sites. The **site** is the basic unit of information to the archaeologist. A site represents any location where there is evidence of meaningful human activity. Sites may be as small as an area of waste flakes left over from the manufacture of stone tools or as large as the Aztec city of Tenochtitlán. **Artifacts** are anything made, modified, or used by humans. They are the product of human behavior. They are the material things people leave behind when a site is abandoned. **Features** are nonportable artifacts which indicate human activity such as burial mounds, storage pits, hearths, or posthole stains from structures. Items such as animal bones, seeds, pollen, charcoal, snails, and fish scales are called **ecofacts**. Ecofacts provide information about the diet of the prehistoric inhabitants at that site and about the prehistoric environment. They can also provide evidence for seasonal occupation.

The **context**, or the relationship of the material remains in time and space, is particularly important. Context lies at the very foundations of modern archaeology and is based on the geological **law of association**. This law states that an artifact is contemporary with the other objects found in the same archaeological horizon or level. Measurements are used to define the position of the object in space and its relationship to other artifacts and features at the site. The time component of context is the date of the object in years or its position in the layers of an archaeological site relative to other artifacts and layers. Items removed from archaeological sites without control on where the objects came from in time and space lose their context and tell us almost nothing.

Archaeologists are somewhat like detectives. They must use artifacts as clues to help solve the mystery of the past. Because an artifact is anything made, modified, or used by humans, it must have been made, modified, or used for a particular function or purpose. It is the archaeologist's job to try to figure out what that function or purpose was. To help determine function, artifacts are classified according to material, color, and shape. Archaeologists also look at locational relationships, or the associations with other artifacts or features found at a site, to suggest function. Some artifacts can be assigned a practical function such as cutting (knife), piercing and killing (spear or arrow point), or carrying and storing (ceramic pot). Other items do not seem to have any known practical use. In these cases, archaeologists then often look to a symbolic, ceremonial, or religious function. That is, material objects may reflect ideas or beliefs. Many things in nature are important in various religions and guide human activities—even such things as planting gardens or hunting animals. Things in nature took on symbolic meaning. Animal shapes, or effigies, expressed in ceramic decoration, carved stones, or earthen mounds were possibly religious **symbols** for prehistoric peoples.

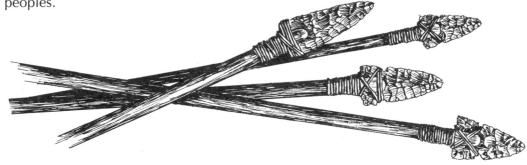

Activity 1. What Is An Artifact?

Age Level   Grades 5–8

Time   30–45 minutes

Focus

Students will understand that an artifact is defined as any object made or utilized by humans. They will understand that the exact function of many artifacts found cannot be known. The students will be able to attempt to identify the possible use of unknown artifacts, utilizing the same interpretive processes archaeologists use.

Equipment

One object *not* familiar to students, three or four objects that may or may not be familiar, and one object that is familiar to students. You may have students each bring an item instead of, or in addition to, items you have collected. Also needed are rulers or measuring tapes, paper or index cards, and pencils or pens. Below is a list of some possible items that could be used, but do not feel limited to this list.

apple peeler	empty shotgun shell	tire iron
curling iron	Christmas tree ornament	Herky the Hawk symbol
spark plug	mortar and pestle	pencil with advertising
empty coke bottle	hurricane lamp	antique nutcracker
old baseball card	plastic cartoon character	garden rake
spool of thread	compass	metal lunch box
matchbook	golf tee	campaign button
rolling pin	silly putty	gavel
deck of cards	music box	Tinkertoy pieces
dog's leash	extension cord	thimble
baby's pacifier	Chiquita banana sticker	dice
TV antenna	staple remover	scissors

Activity Preparation

Discuss with the students the fact that the basis of any science is the ability to describe observations. Emphasize that descriptions should include size, shape, color, the type of construction material (glass, plastic, wood, or stone), and method of construction (hand made vs. machine made). In archaeology, size descriptions must include actual measurements.

Activity

1. This activity can either be done as a large group activity or with the students divided into smaller groups of four to six students (Step 1). Create an index card or separate sheet of paper for each object recording descriptions (Step 2), descriptive name (Step 3), and possible uses (Step 4).
2. Have students describe each object (or list the object's attributes).

3. Have the group come up with names for the objects based on the descriptions. Quite often an artifact is given a name based on its descriptive qualities because its use is unknown.

4. Have the group discuss how the objects might be used based on their attributes. For example, if the object has a sharp edge, it could have been used for cutting.

5. If the activity is done in small groups, have groups share their descriptions. Can members of the other groups add to the descriptions, offer suggestions of other descriptive names, or provide ideas about possible uses?

6. Many of the items archaeologists find have no parallel in modern society, and archaeologists are unable to discover their original function. Introduce the familiar objects, discuss how they are used in our culture, and then discuss possible alternate uses based on descriptive attributes that someone from another culture or an archaeologist a thousand years from now might provide. How might the archaeologist be able to infer the correct function of the items? With what other items were they found? In what kind of structure or feature were they found? What possible uses could be suggested based on the items' descriptive attributes? Sometimes archaeologists will attempt to determine the function or the method of production of an artifact through experimentation. They may try to reproduce, or replicate, the artifacts using materials and tools available to the cultural group under study. They may also try using the artifact for the function suggested by the item's attributes or similarity to a contemporary object. For example, can the artifact be used for slicing, cutting, scraping, puncturing, clasping, sitting on, or storing liquids or solids?

Activity 2. Symbolic Versus Practical Objects

Age Level   Grades 5–8

Time   30–45 minutes

Focus

The student will understand the difference between practical and "symbolic" objects. The student will understand that the meaning of symbolic objects may vary from person to person and certainly from culture to culture.

Equipment

See suggestions under Activity Preparation below. Select several items or photographs of items from the listed examples. Also needed are magazines, picture books, paper, and pencils.

Activity Preparation

Discuss with the students the difference between ritual or symbolic versus practical objects. The dictionary defines a symbol as "something used for or regarded as representing something else; a material object representing something, often something immaterial; emblem, token, or sign." Discuss symbols from geographic places or religious symbols. Other widely recognized symbols such as those for poison or international traffic could also be discussed. Examples may include: Iowa symbols—prairie rose, goldfinch, ear of corn; national symbols—Liberty Bell, American Eagle, Canadian maple leaf; traffic or danger symbols—poison, international traffic symbols; advertising symbols—Pillsbury doughboy, McDonald's golden arches; school mascots—Hawkeyes, Cyclones, Panthers; religious symbols—cross, Star of David. As part of the discussion, you could show students pictures of various symbols and see if they can recognize their meaning.

Activity

1. Ask each student to make a list of 10 objects in each category—symbolic and practical, e.g., flag and shovel. This could also be done in either small or large groups.
2. You could have students look through magazines and books for symbolic objects. Also have them look around their environment for symbols—in their school or town. Have them share their findings with each other. Have the students consider how many of the symbols have national or worldwide recognition and how many would have meaning only to a smaller group—state or local recognition. What are some reasons (TV, ready availability of books, newspapers, magazines, widespread travel) certain symbols might be recognized nation-wide or world-wide?
3. Ask students to think of events which have meaning in our culture but which might have a different meaning or no meaning in another culture. Examples might be: July 4, Thanksgiving, Washington's birthday, Super Bowl Sunday, and Columbus Day. Point out that American Indians certainly have a different view of Columbus from the mainstream American view.

Extensions

1. Students could select an animal figure of significance to them and construct their own out of clay, wood, or soil. In winter, have the class try to construct effigy mounds in the snow. Have other class members try to guess what animals the mounds represent.

2. Tell students about recognized prehistoric symbols—long-nosed god mask, the weeping eye motif. Use Lennis Moore's illustration of a long-nosed god mask in Duane Anderson's *Western Iowa Prehistory*. The complete reference is listed in the back of this book. The weeping eye motif is shown below. Examples of prehistoric effigies and totems could be shown and discussed.

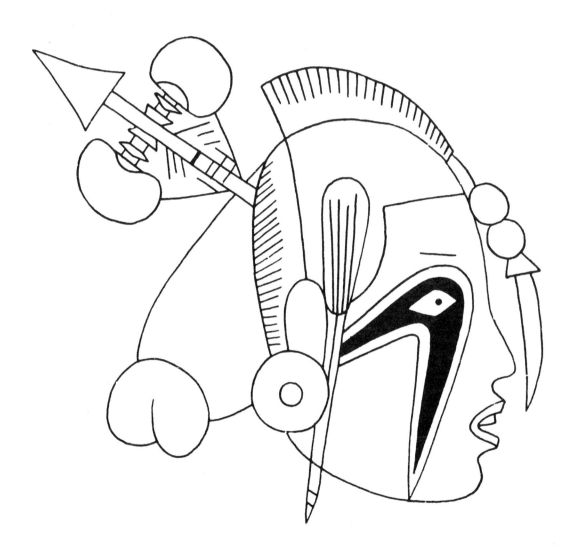

Profile of a dancer wearing ceremonial costuming and painted with the weeping eye motif. Archaeologists now believe the weeping eye represents the characteristic plumage markings on the head and neck of the peregrine falcon.

The Work of Archaeologists

Archaeologists are frequently asked, "how do you know where to dig"? The "where" is a matter of finding archaeological sites through one of two ways—survey and accidental discovery. Accidental discoveries occur when activities such as construction, farming, and erosion uncover bones, stone artifacts, ceramics, charcoal, or ashes. A **survey** is a deliberate search of an area for sites and can involve surface inspection, subsurface testing, remote sensing, and aerial photography. A survey may be complete, or it may sample an area. Once sites are found and a research design developed, studies of settlement pattern and resource use can be conducted with the survey data, or specific sites may be selected for excavation based on their potential to answer specific research questions. Often, an excavation is conducted on a site slated for destruction by road or building construction to evaluate the site's importance or to salvage as much archaeological information as possible before the site is destroyed.

Excavation is the primary technique of archaeological recovery. The nature of the excavation is dependent upon the site itself, available time, and funding. Usually only a sample of the site is excavated, with part of the site left for future archaeologists. Research designs are geared to recover data which will help solve specific problems or questions. The types of questions influence the specific recovery methods used. Excavation can be horizontal, opening up large areas looking for house structures or village features. Excavation can also be vertical such as when a trench is dug across a site. A vertical trench can give the archaeologist a quick overview of the **stratification** or the layering of deposits at the site. The stratification provides information about the sequence of occupation.

Excavation is a destructive process. At the same time you are recovering data you are destroying the site. Therefore, meticulous recording of the archaeological findings becomes essential. Before any digging begins, archaeologists divide the site with a **grid** or a series of square excavation units. Each unit is dug in levels. Everything found in a particular grid unit must be labeled with the **site number**, unit number and level, excavator's name, and date. The grid helps the archaeologist keep track of the location of everything found at a site.

Archaeologists use various tools and equipment to excavate—shovels, trowels, dental picks, tweezers, soft brush, string, line level, metric tape measure, buckets, bags, note forms, and map forms. If nothing is visible on the surface of the square, the first tool that would be used to actually dig would be a shovel. Archaeologists do not dig large chunks; instead, they carefully skim off thin layers. When they reach anything buried in the dirt, archaeologists switch to a small flat-bladed trowel which allows careful excavation of the dirt from around objects without damaging them. The excavated soil is also screened through a wire-mesh screen to recover small items that might be missed by shovel skimming or troweling alone.

Objects are never yanked out of an excavation unit. Their relationships to other objects in the unit must be noted. Changes in soil color must also be noted. Dark stains within lighter-colored soil could indicate a feature such as a posthole stain, a hearth, or a storage pit. Archaeologists keep records of everything found in the unit. Archaeologists map on a piece of graph paper the location of artifacts, bones, and features found at each level in the unit.

To recover very small items, such as seeds, nut shells, fish scales, and very small animal bones, a soil sample is removed from the unit. The soil is gently poured in water and stirred. Any item lighter than water will float to the top and can be poured out onto a fine screen. This process is called **flotation**.

A second question frequently asked of archaeologists is, "How can you tell how old something is?" In archaeology, we are talking about long periods of time (hundreds and thousands of years) rather than short periods of time (days and weeks). There are two basic types of dating in archaeology—relative dating and absolute dating. **Relative dating** tells us the order of something in relation to something else, the arranging of materials in sequence—older or younger. The two main methods used in relative dating are stratigraphy and seriation. **Stratigraphy**, or the actual sequence of events at a site, provides information about the association of artifacts and features relative to one another in time. To date events by means of stratigraphy, archaeologists use the **law of superposition**, which states that the materials found below other items are assumed to have been deposited first and are therefore older. Unless something has happened to disturb the natural order of deposition, the youngest or most recent remains will be those first encountered. **Seriation** is based on the assumption that the use of certain artifact types goes through a period of rising popularity, reaches a peak, and finally declines in popularity. Similar frequencies of certain artifact types found at several sites suggests that those sites are probably contemporary.

Absolute dating provides the age of something in years. Organic remains in the form of charred wood, bone, and shell are important in determining the age of the site. Such material can be subjected to the most familiar technique of absolute dating, the radiocarbon method. When anything living dies, it begins to lose the radioactive carbon that it contains. This loss can be measured. The smaller the amount of radioactive carbon, the older the artifact or material being tested. Radiocarbon analysis can tell within a certain range of years, the probable age of organic materials, and thus, the time of occupation of the site. Other techniques used in absolute dating include dendrochronology or tree-ring dating, potassium-argon dating, obsidian hydration, and thermoluminescence. For additional information on these techniques, consult the references listed in the back of this book.

After a site is excavated, laboratory processing begins. Cultural materials recovered must be washed, labeled with a unique catalog number to preserve locational information, and then sorted. Careful analysis is required to interpret the prehistoric activities at that site and their significance.

Archaeology has borrowed a number of techniques from various fields and incorporates an interdisciplinary approach. Most archaeologists become specialists in a specific area and time period, and often in a particular aspect such as ceramics, lithics, subsistence, faunal remains, floral remains, settlement patterns, or ecology. They often work with specialists in other fields such as paleobotany (plants), vertebrate osteology (animal bones), palynology (pollen), and geomorphology (landforms and soils). For example, working with a geomorphologist can be valuable. This scientist can date a soil deposit, making it possible to date the archaeological deposit found in it. A geomorphologist can also help archaeologists know where to look for sites by knowing the age of the landforms present. They can also help archaeologists determine if there are gaps in the archaeological record by determining where archaeological sites may have been destroyed due to geological processes.

The following illustrates the type of archaeological evidence that can be recovered from an excavation of a prehistoric house or village. In Iowa, you would not find whole houses still standing after a thousand years. The houses would have disappeared a long time ago. What remains are small dark circles in the ground called **post molds**, representing what was once the wall of a house. From the arrangement of these post molds, archaeologists can determine the size and shape of the house and how the house may have been constructed. What causes post molds? During the building of a house, a hole is dug and a post set in the hole. At some later time, if the post begins to rot or burns down, the base will still remain in the ground. Eventually the base would also decay and leave an area of darker soil. This is finally covered by more dirt and plants.

Other archaeological evidence can include cache or storage pits. Archaeologists think that such pits were used to store food, keeping it safe in a sealed underground chamber. A cache pit was made by first digging a hole in the ground, lining it with grass, and then filling it with corn or other food items. When the food had been removed and consumed, the empty pit was filled with garbage and covered over, remaining in the ground and preserving a record of the past. Plant and animal remains recovered from these pits can provide information on the diet of the prehistoric occupants of the site, as well as information on environmental conditions.

Two different colors of soil side by side are also clues telling where a house had been located. Usually the area that had been inside the house will have a darker soil color than the area outside due to a higher content of decayed organic material.

Right. A cache pit seen in cross section. Corn, beans, and squash were often stored for use during the winter in such a pit. After being filled, it was sealed to keep out water and rodents.

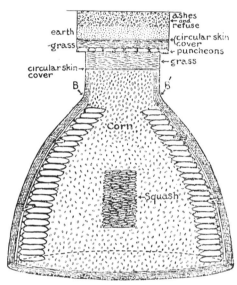

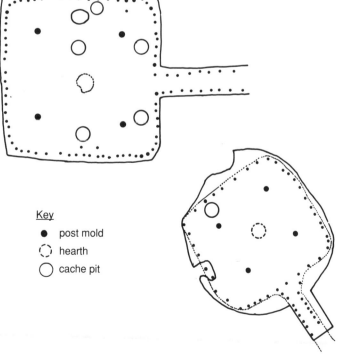

Key

● post mold
◌ hearth
○ cache pit

Left. The archaeological remains of two prehistoric houses found in southwestern Iowa. People entered the houses through long, narrow entryways.

Activity 3. Picnic Ground Archaeology

Age Level   Grade 5–8

Time   Best accomplished over 2–3 hours or two to three class periods.

Focus

The students will understand how archaeologists gather information by collecting material from the surface of the ground. They will be able to record the exact location of material found and understand why knowing that exact location is necessary. They will be able to interpret some past activities based on the material collected. This is a form of archaeological information gathering via surface collection.

Equipment

Survey flags, large paper or plastic garbage bags, zip lock bags, permanent felt-tip marker, old tooth brushes, plastic tubs, water, notebooks or writing paper, pencils, graph paper, and clip-boards. (Survey flags can be ordered from Forestry Suppliers, Inc., P.O. Box 8397, Jackson, MS, 39284-8397, or possibly obtained from your local county engineer or soil conservation office.)

Activity Preparation

Discuss the modern uses of picnic grounds. Consider why we have picnic grounds; consider activities that take place on the grounds; consider who uses the grounds and when. Discuss the archaeologist's job of information gathering via surface collection. Discuss the various methods involved in conducting an archaeological surface collection; choose site to be surface collected.

Activity

1. Have the students collect material from the ground surface, limiting the time to 30 minutes.
    a. Give each student a handful of survey flags.
    b. Line students up at 3–4 feet intervals along one edge of area to be surveyed.
    c. Have them slowly and carefully walk forward, examining the ground for any "garbage." When anything is found, stick a flag in the ground next to the item. Do not have the student pick up the item at this time.
    d. When the group gets to the other side of the picnic ground, have the line of students rotate around the inside end person so they are now facing the opposite direction at the same spacing interval. Proceed as in Step c. Continue until the whole area has been covered.
    e. Have the students make a sketch map of the picnic area showing the location of each flag. Number or assign a letter to each flag and corresponding artifact. Make sure each number or letter appears on the map. As each flagged artifact is mapped, place the artifact in a separate bag marked with the appropriate number or letter. Pull the flag before proceeding to the next flagged artifact.
    f. Gather all items recovered at the end of the collection period so all students can see the range of items—duplicates, one of a kinds, foreign, or unknowns. Then return to class.
    g. Have students begin to think about the items collected in relation to the modern use discussed in preparation for the activity.

2. Have the students identify and classify all material recovered.
   a. Clean up items, keeping identification number or letter by using yellow stick-on tags, marker, or index cards, and display on tables with adequate space.
   b. Identify as many as possible and begin to group like items together.
   c. Record and count items as totals and as groups. Use the sketch map.
   d. Discuss the items in relation to what they are, where on the grounds they were found, what this tells us about the activities and users of the picnic grounds.
3. Discuss the activity with the students.
   a. What did you learn from the items alone, the various groups of items, and their locations within the grounds?
   b. What can be said with relative certainty about the picnic ground use?
   c. What incorrect assumptions may be made from the recovered items and the related questions and their answers?
   d. What could you have done differently or additionally to gain a better understanding of the grounds?
   e. How would your inferences change if you had not had first hand knowledge of picnics and picnic grounds?

Note: This activity is a good lead-in to the aquarium or simulated dig because excavation is the next step in information gathering used by the archaeologist. Classroom activities appropriate at this time may be public TV programs, films, or readings on archaeology. Also, scientific methods can be discussed or greater detail given if already discussed. The garbage studies by the University of Arizona are ideal for a synopsis of this activity and a lead into the next. See two articles on this type of study by William R. Rathje (see page 41). Garbage studies also tie in nicely with a discussion of landfill problems, biodegradable disposables, and recycling.

Extensions

1. Obtain sample Site Record Sheets by writing to the Office of the State Archaeologist (OSA). The OSA will also send you information on how to fill out the sheets. Then make a copy for each student or group of students. Have each student or group select some location where evidence of some modern human activity has been left—thus, by definition, selecting a potential site. Each student should then fill out a site sheet giving the information that might be useful to an archaeologist. Have each student try to locate one of his or her classmate's sites using the Site Record Sheet. (This activity could also be used with the section on "Archaeological Ethics and Law.")
2. Make a list of the things your household disposes of in a day's garbage. What could an archaeologist learn about your lifestyle by examining this garbage?
3. Ask the students if their house, room, or garbage reveal the same kind of evidence as their neighbor's house, room, or garbage. How might the evidence left be different? How would it be the same? Compare and contrast the archaeological evidence that might be found for the following buildings—a school, different types of stores, and a church.
4. Make a list of different aspects of life today—family, work, play, school, travel, and religion. Then have students decide what objects might give future archaeologists clues to the details of these aspects of modern life. Students should soon begin to realize that some of the aspects may be more difficult to represent by tangible objects and to understand that archaeologists today may be missing some information about prehistoric people and also may be misinterpreting the information they do have.

*Activity 4. Garbage Can Archaeology**

Age Level   Grades 3–8

Time   1 hour

Focus

The students will learn the idea of using stratigraphy to date objects by understanding that the material at the bottom of the basket was thrown in first.

Equipment

Two or more wastebaskets from the school filled with trash. The teacher should select wastebaskets from rooms that will show clear-cut, interpretable differences. Wastebaskets from a classroom or two, possibly from different grades, could be contrasted with ones from the cafeteria, gymnasium, library, and offices.

Activity Preparation

Collect wastebaskets from the several predetermined locations. Gather the students and carefully go through the wastebasket from your classroom. Discuss the meaning of the trash and ask the students questions such as: What items do you think were placed in the wastebasket first and which last? By using only the trash, what can be learned about the activities that have taken place in this room?

Activity

Divide the students into groups and have each group sort through a different wastebasket using the principles of stratigraphy. One idea to show that the top layer is the most recent and the bottom the oldest would be to take the groups outside and draw the wastebasket on the sidewalk with chalk. With chalk, divide the wastebasket into three layers. The children are to put the top third of the garbage in the top layer, the second in the middle, and the last third in the bottom layer. Next, the artifacts can be categorized. Then have the students decide the original location (provenience) of each wastebasket. Remember, don't tell the students where the wastebaskets originated!

Extension

This activity can also be a good exercise in making inferences about a culture from material remains. It can be used as a springboard to discussions on the cultural basis of our knowledge about artifacts. Most of the students' inferences will require already knowing how a given thing functions in our society: if you did not have that knowledge, how would it affect your conclusions? How would you go about getting that knowledge? (See discussions in activities "What is an Artifact" and "Picnic Ground Archaeology.")

Have students make an actual list of items from the garbage can and their possible uses. Then ask the students to consider these questions:

What kind of life does this inventory suggest?
What goods are used by which members of this society or group?
In what economic and social arrangements would these materials be used?

14

What can be deduced from the evidence?
How complete an inventory of all the material used is represented in the remains of this garbage can, i.e., what material used would *not* show up in the garbage?

*Adapted from a lesson plan by the same title prepared by E. Charles Adams, Arizona State Museum, and Barbara Groneman, Southwest Learning Sources, appearing in U.S. National Park Service Archaeological Assistance Program, Technical Brief No. 4, May 1989.

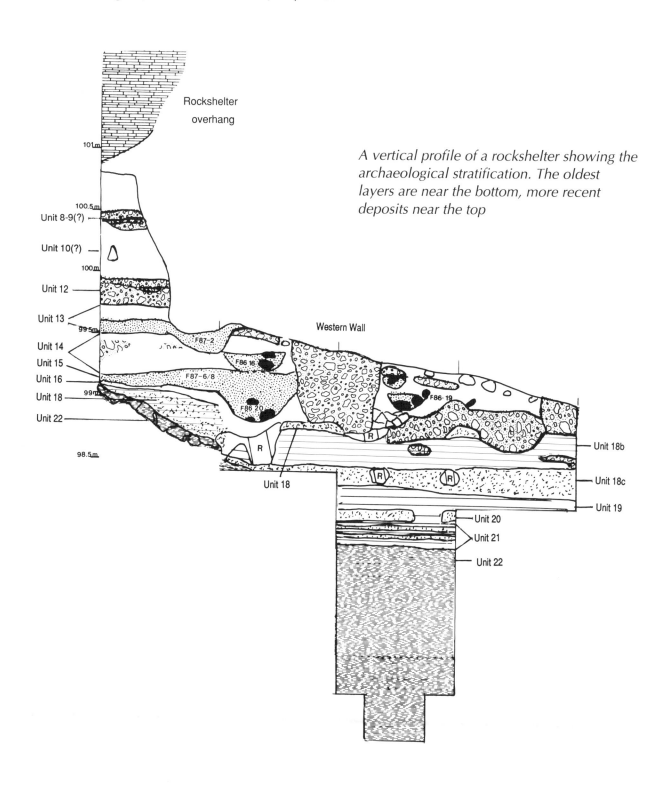

A vertical profile of a rockshelter showing the archaeological stratification. The oldest layers are near the bottom, more recent deposits near the top

Activity 5. Simulated Archaeological Dig*

Age Level Grade 5–8

Time 1½–2 hours

Focus

The student will understand one of the very basic principles of stratigraphy, that objects or material buried earliest will be deepest and those buried latest will be on top. On a very elementary level, they will be able to understand correct excavation procedure. They will be able to take simple field notes and sketch artifacts.

Equipment

A meter square frame made of 1 x 6's that can set on the ground (a sand box, aquarium, or any other relatively large-sized container where several students can work together will also suffice). Three different types of "soil" for the different levels (for example, kitty litter, sand, and garden dirt), artifacts for three levels (see list below), trowels, brushes, dental picks (optional), meter square grid (see directions below), graph paper, clip boards, pencils, and Elmer's glue.

Below is a list of suggested items that could be used, but do not feel limited to this list. Items for each level though should be related to each other in some way—same time period and associated with a particular activity or set of activities. Using only parts of items or broken items will more closely simulate the incompleteness of archaeological remains.

Modern
swimming pool or picnic area:
  plastic pop rings
  small potato chip bag
  suntan lotion bottle
  sun glasses
  pop can
  ice cream stick
kitchen items:
  wire whisk
  spoon
  broken glass or dish
office supply items:
  paper clips
  scissors
  pencils.

Turn of Century
objects suggesting a farm:
  barbed wire
  rake head
  broken, older-looking dishes
  broken antique bottle
  cow bones

Prehistoric Iowa
small imitation projectile points
fire cracked rock
broken animal bones
fresh water mussel shells
hammerstone

Directions for making the grid: Inner dimensions equal 1-meter square (or whatever size unit you will be using). Drill holes through frame horizontally at 10-cm intervals using inner dimensions. Thread heavy string through holes forming grid.

Activity Preparation

Create the "site" to be excavated in advance. Discuss archaeological excavations and techniques. (Instructors review text on pages 8–9.) Why and where do archaeologists excavate? What do archaeologists hope to learn from an excavation? How do they dig (tools needed, excavation plan, recording methods, and collection and storage methods)? Where in the ground would the oldest artifacts be found? Where would the youngest be found? Devise an excavation plan to be used for the simulated dig. Discuss the tools, excavation methods, and recording methods to use.

Activity

1. Divide students into teams for the excavation and have a plan for who is responsible for what during the activity. Depending upon the size of the class, students can be divided into three groups, each assigned to a different stratigraphic level. The groups can be further subdivided by assigning some students to be excavators, some recorders, and some lab technicians.
2. Carefully uncover artifacts found in the upper stratigraphic layer, using correct archaeological procedures. Take field notes to identify artifacts and their placement.
3. Place the grid you made over the exposed artifacts and sketch to scale their original positions on graph paper.
4. Remove the artifacts to a sturdy paper bag, plastic bag, or box, mark the bag or box as to the stratigraphic layer from which the items came.
5. Repeat Steps 2–4 for the other two stratigraphic layers.
6. Take the bags or boxes of artifacts to the "lab." At the "lab," the group will list and categorize all the artifacts found.
7. In each level, there should be some artifacts that can be reconstructed, such as a pottery bowl, dish, or old bottle. The group should attempt to put the artifact back together using glue. If a few pieces of the broken item are missing, it will be more like the real thing.
8. At the conclusion, have each group share inferences about the artifacts they found and support their conclusion with observations they made.

Extensions

1. If there are any abandoned farmsteads in your area, have the students do a careful examination of the materials and structures at the site, possibly preparing a map of where everything was found. Then from the map and their observations, have the students try to reconstruct the way of life. They should be able to refer to specifics from the farmstead to support their ideas. This activity should involve surface inspection, collection, and mapping only. You should not attempt to have students excavate a real archaeological site.
2. Take the students to a stream bank, road cut, or limestone exposure to discuss stratigraphic principles of layering—oldest to most recent. Relate that to layering at an archaeological site.
3. Find examples of the "grid system" in everyday life such as maps or cities that are laid out in even squares.
4. Break a flower pot, cup, or plate and mix up the pieces. Have students try to restore the object. Some of the pieces could be left out simulating the experience of actual archaeologists trying to restore bones or pottery. This could be set up as a competition between teams.

*Adapted from an activity entitled "An Archaeological Dig" prepared by Gail B. Wortmann, Ottumwa High School, and used for a young people's summer workshop program in 1989, sponsored by the Exploratorium of Iowa, Ottumwa.

Pottery

Ceramics are an example of one very important artifact for the archaeologist. They are breakable yet almost indestructible, so they occur in abundance after hundreds of years in the ground. They were also an avenue of artistic expression. Prehistoric potters formed and decorated their vessels in a variety of ways. Other potters in, and sometimes outside, their community then copied these designs. Because these styles were traded among groups, archaeologists are often able to relate sites in time and space because they contain the same ceramic types.

When ceramics are uncovered at a site, they usually occur as small broken pieces or **sherds**. Occasionally, all of the fragments of the vessel will have survived, and the pot can be reconstructed, just as you might work a jigsaw puzzle. Sometimes when only a portion of a former pot is left, the rest can be rebuilt with plaster of Paris if enough remains to provide some idea of the original shape and size.

The appearance of pottery during Woodland times approximately 2,500 years ago is significant because it indicates that people may have become more sedentary. Earlier peoples used lightweight, portable skin bags or carried woven containers made from inner bark of trees or reeds. Nomadic hunters and gatherers would not have wanted to carry heavy breakable pots. When they began to settle in villages for parts of the year, however, they found many uses for pottery.

Pottery vessels were made from local clays to which sand, crushed stone, ground mussel shell, crushed fired clay, or plant fibers had been added for **temper**. The temper prevented shrinkage and cracking during firing or drying.

Pots were made prehistorically by several methods: coiling, paddling, or pinching and shaping. In coiling, the potter rolls a lump of clay into a coil and gradually builds up the vessel wall by adding more coils. Each coiled layer is pinched to the one beneath and the coils are subsequently thinned by squeezing between the potter's thumbs and fingers. The coil junctures can then be smoothed. Studies of prehistoric ceramics found in Iowa indicate pottery here was made by paddling or by pinching and shaping. A lump of clay was pounded into shape by holding the clay against a large stone and paddling it with a wooden paddle. If the paddle was covered with woven fabric or cord, the patterned markings appeared on the clay. The lump of clay might also be pinched and shaped by hand. Sometimes designs like lines and triangles were scribed into the clay before it was fired.

Gradually the styles and decorations changed. A greater variety of pots—bowls, pans, jars, and water bottles—were made for different functions. Pots were used for both storage and cooking. Sometimes tiny toy pots were made for or by children.

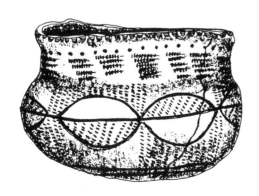
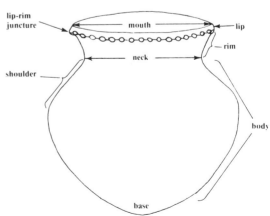

Activity 6. Pottery Making

Age Level   Grades 5–8

Time   30–45 minutes

Focus

Students will learn about prehistoric pottery making techniques by experimenting with their own attempts. They will gain an appreciation of the skill of early potters.

Equipment

Clay, either purchased potter's clay or clay collected from a natural source such as a nearby creek bank, tempering agent (sand, finely crushed rock, burned and crushed freshwater mussel shell), twine or cord, loosely woven fabric such as burlap, sticks or pencils, boards or pieces of heavy cardboard for each student.

Activity Preparation

Discuss tempering, pass out the selected tempering agent, and have the students place it on their board. If you are using burned shell, point out differences between burned and unburned—color, ease of crushing. To burn clam shell, place directly in a bed of coals for an hour or more. When cool, the shells should crush easily and be blue-gray in appearance. If you choose to have the students use clay from a natural source, check the banks of a stream or creek. Clay comes in different colors in different regions of the state. It may be red, yellow, white, blue, or gray, but it is distinct in color from the topsoil. Sample the material by taking a handful and mashing it together. If it holds without crumbling, it probably has a high clay content. Clay taken at or just above the water level will probably be moist enough to work without further processing. It will stay workable for some time if sealed in a plastic bag or plastic container. If the clay is too dry to work, it must be dried out completely, broken up, and reconstituted with water until the right consistency is reached. Commercial clay can also be purchased.

Activity

1. Give each student a handful of clay. Have students roll clay in temper and knead; continue until clay is workable. This is similar to adding flour to a dough; if you add too much, the mixture will become too stiff to work.
2. Slam the clay onto the boards to remove air bubbles.
3. Shape into a ball and tap on hard surface to form a cube.
4. Holding clay in hands, use thumbs to push center down and out and use fingers to pull clay up and in, thus forming the pot.
5. If the student is not happy with the results, go back to Step 3 and try again.
6. If small cracks develop while shaping the pot, dip finger lightly in water and rub into crack (use sparingly). Use the finger and thumb to mend cracks.
7. Divide the class into groups of four or five students. Have the groups each decide on a way to decorate their pots. Here are some examples of techniques that might be used for decoration:

a. Wrap a stick or paddle with cord and use it to shape a thin pot, giving the outer surface of the pot a cord-marked appearance.

b. While clay is still wet, add additional decorations by impressing a single cord into the clay, wrapping the pot in burlap or other loosely-woven fabric and pressing it gently into the clay, or using your finger or a stick to push small depressions into the clay.

c. Let the pot air dry for about 10 minutes. Then thin and shape walls using an unburned mussel shell. Scrape out the bumps. It's like shaving, be careful to avoid nicks and cuts.

d. Use a sharpened stick or pencil to scribe geometric designs into neck and shoulder of the pot.

e. Add effigies to the pot by molding a small amount of clay into an animal shape and attaching it as a handle to the pot.

8. Compare the designs from the various groups. How are they alike? How are they different?

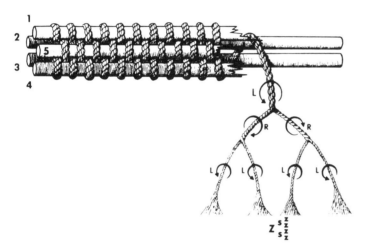

A paddle, used for decorating pots, made of several sticks wrapped with cordage

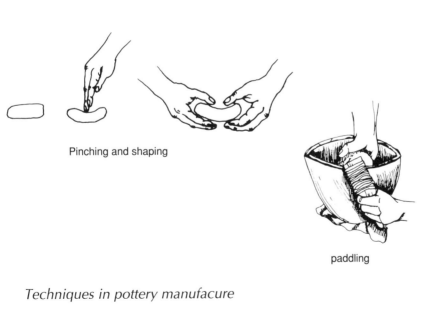

Pinching and shaping

paddling

Techniques in pottery manufacure

coiling

Prehistoric Use of Natural Resources for Tools, Shelter, and Food

Plant and animal remains left by prehistoric people are found at some sites. Earlier archaeologists discarded these kinds of data not realizing their importance in interpreting prehistoric cultures. Today, we know that all data are important, especially those which tell us about the prehistoric environment and the diets of early peoples. Some evidence can also indicate the time of year a site was occupied. For example, a deer sheds its antlers during the winter. If a deer skull is found with shed antlers and no new antler growth, archaeologists would know the deer was killed during the winter.

From the standpoint of human adaptation, patterns of local vegetation are of crucial concern. Open prairie would have been attractive for its grasses, bison, and prairie wildfowl like the ruffed grouse, quail, and prairie chicken. The contact zone between prairie grassland and deciduous forest supported a variety of plants and animals. In early summer, tender new plants and leaves would have been attractive to hunters and the game they pursued. Some of the wild plants collected for leaves or seeds included goosefoot, pigweed, marsh elder, and knotweed. Sumac, plums, chokecherries, grapes, and raspberries would also have been abundant at the forest edge. Women probably utilized these fruits in a variety of teas and cakes, and probably mixed them with fat and meat to form pemmican. Some of the fruits may have been dried and stored for use later in the year. The roots and bark of many plants also had medicinal uses.

The walnuts, hickory nuts, and acorns which grew in the forest proper provided food for both humans and animals. We can look to **ethnographic accounts**, or written accounts of historic Indian groups, to guess at the many ways these foods may have been used by prehistoric peoples. Nuts were probably eaten raw, cooked in soups, and powdered to form a thickening agent. Most acorns had to be leached to extract the bitter tannic acid. In historic times, a black dye was made from the root of the black walnut. The bark of some trees was the ingredient for medications, and sap from trees like the maple and box elder were used for sugar. The forest would also have provided materials for shelters, firewood, and wood for tools and bowls.

Dependable, renewable plant resources also were found along the rivers. Among these were the arrow leaf plant, yellow lotus, and wild rice. The root of the arrow leaf was boiled or roasted, while both the roots and the hard, nutlike seed of the yellow lotus were mixed with meat and cooked. Yellow lotus roots were also dried and stored for winter use. Rushes and reeds along the river's edge were raw materials for baskets, cordage, and fabric. River valleys would have hosted a variety of large and small game, turtles, fishes, mollusks, and large numbers of migratory waterfowl during spring and fall. In addition to providing food, various bones from these animals were made into tools and ornaments such as awls, needles, scapula hoes, fish hooks, beads, and bracelets. Fur from animals made excellent clothing and blankets. The shells from freshwater mussels were made into spoons, scoops, beads, and other ornaments.

Hunting was a means of getting food, clothing, and other necessities. Cooperative hunts would have been essential for successful bison kills, since bison roamed in herds, as large as several thousand animals. A number of hunters would have had to work together. One way might have been to sneak up on the grazing animals. Then, frightened by shouting, waving blankets, or thrown spears, the bison would stampede over the edge of a small cliff or ravine and be easily killed. If bison were grazing on flat plains, a large group of people might work together to surround the bison. This would take many more people and more planning than killing more solitary animals such as moose, elk, or deer. The hunting of these animals possibly involved cooperative efforts of small hunting parties, but with the advent of the bow and arrow approximately 1,400 years ago, lone hunters could successfully stalk these animals.

Smaller animals were also trapped. The deadfall trap was made with one end of a heavy log supported by a sharp stick with bait attached. The lower end of this upright was set on a short stick which was displaced when the upright was moved. Smaller animals could be caught using snares. One such snare used twisted deer hide thongs for a noose and was hung from a tree. To reach the bait, the animal had to put its head through the loop.

Waterfowl could be killed in great numbers at molting seasons when they could not fly. Men armed with clubs would wade into the water and strike them down. Fish could be obtained using nets, spears, or fish hooks made from bone. Occasionally remnants of **fish weirs** are found. Weirs were large sieves made of sticks and a rock foundation which would trap the fish but allow the water to continue flowing.

Some of the meat and fish would have been consumed immediately. Some would have been dried or smoked for later use.

For much of the prehistoric past, fruits and vegetables in the diet were supplied solely by collecting wild plants. About 4,000 years ago or more, however, people started cultivating plants. No one knows exactly why and how farming began, but by a thousand years ago crops like corn, beans, squash, and sunflowers had become an important part of the diet of these early people. The early farming fields were small—more like gardens—and probably provided only a part of the food the people needed. It is likely women took care of the growing of plants while the men continued hunting.

Farming allowed people to live in one place for a longer time, allowing them to build more permanent houses. They would not have to be moving as much to hunt for new food plants. In fact, they would need to stay in one place longer—to plant the seeds, take care of the young plants, and harvest the crops. With the food supply more certain, the land could support more people. People began establishing large villages. Farming changed the way of life. No longer was everyone living in small hunting groups and moving often.

Where were the people planting their crops? Much of Iowa was covered with prairie grasses that have thick, tough roots. Today farmers can cut through the roots with steel plows, making long furrows in which to plant their seeds. The early farmer would not have had such strong tools. Most likely these early farmers grew their crops in small gardens planted near their homes in forest clearings or near the forest edge. Land was probably cleared using fire. Fire may also have helped fell even large trees. If the base of the trees were burned, then stone axes could cut away the charred part until the tree fell.

Once the land was cleared, various tools were used for gardening: a scoop made from a bison skull or horn core, a sharpened, fire-hardened digging stick, or a scapula hoe. Hoes, made from the shoulder blade of animals like the bison, are common tools found on prehistoric farming sites. The bones were slightly trimmed in order to make it easier to attach them to a wooden handle. Many deer jaws found on some farming sites had their lower edges cut in a similar way. Some archaeologists believe these were attached to handles and used like sickles to cut tall grasses.

Activity 7. Resources for Tools and Shelter

Age Level   Grades 5–8

Time   30–45 minutes

Focus

Students will become more aware of the natural resources around them, how prehistoric people may have used these resources, and how they themselves could use these same resources to survive.

Equipment

Papers, pencils, natural materials from which to make tool kits.

Activity Preparation

Discuss what types of natural resources are available locally, now or in the past, that could be used to provide or construct shelters (rockshelters or caves; young trees and bark for shelters) and to make tools (different types of rock; young trees for tool handles, bows, arrows, spear shafts; clay for pottery; reeds and fibers for weaving baskets or bags; animal bones for needles, awls, fishhooks, garden hoes). Also stress the importance of having a close, reliable source of water.

Activity

1. Divide the class into small groups. Then assign each group one task that prehistoric people would have had to do to survive (hunting, fishing trip, gathering wild plants or nuts, planting garden, building fires, clearing land, and building a house). Have each group plan the activity carefully, considering how the labor will be divided and how they are going to accomplish the task.
2. Then have the group plan a tool kit necessary to accomplish that task using only the materials that would have been available in the natural environment. If possible, have the group try to construct one of the tools in the kit.
3. Have the groups present their tool kits to the class for suggestions and then have each group report to the class on how they would accomplish their activity. They might also role play a part of the activity.

Extensions

1. Hike in a county park. Look at what is available to make a shelter, what kinds of stone and other material can be found to make tools and other items you would need to survive (other than food). Examples might be wood, stone, bone, or clay.
2. Have students design houses that prehistoric people might have built. They should think about the kind of tools they would have had as well as the locally available raw materials. Then ask them to build a scale model of their house or to submit detailed plans.
3. If open areas are available, send a group of students out into a forested area and another group out into a prairie area. Ask each group to evaluate the landscape in terms of how they would live. What materials are available for tools, what kinds of plants grow wild or could be cultivated, what kind of animal habitat is it? Bring the two groups back together and have

them compare their evaluations. Have them list the advantages and disadvantages of each habitat type.

4. If land is available in a nearby park or open ground, have groups of students scout to find the best sites to:

   a. build a house (take into consideration shelter from wind, sunlight, drainage, proximity to water, and whether the shelter will be used only seasonally or year-round),

   b. plant a garden,

   c. hunt for wild plants, and

   d. hunt various kinds of animals.

   Have each group report to the class and explain their choices. Compare results.

5. If you can acquire some animal bones, have your students experiment making bone tools. Use Morrow's "Bone Tools" in Appendix C as a guide. Local farmers may be a source of cow bone. Deer bone or bone from large birds such as turkey may also be used. Make sure the bone is aged and free of flesh.

W. Thomson '93

Activity 8. Resources for Food

Age Level   Grades 5–8

Time   1–3 hours

Focus

The students will begin to think of the environment in a new way—as a source of their basic human needs.

Equipment

Photographs of, or information on, the wild plants and animals native to the area. Field guides to edible wild plants. Utensils, plates, and cooking equipment needed if class will be preparing meal. Poster board and other supplies if students will be making posters.

Activity Preparation

Ask the students where they could go to get food if there were no grocery stores. Hunting and fishing would be a simple and obvious source of meat. Collecting plants would be a good way to obtain the nutritionally necessary fruits and vegetables.

Activity

1. Have the students research what edible plants and animals are available around your area of Iowa. Make a list, which could include such items as birds, fish, deer, and a multitude of edible plants. If possible, hike in county parks and look at what is available for food. Then have the class plan a meal using only the resources locally available. If possible, have the class prepare the meal, smaller groups taking charge of the various dishes. Examples: milk weed blossoms, young cattail heads, mushrooms, berries, wild asparagus, and nuts. The field guides to edible wild plants listed in the references contain preparation suggestions for many of the plants. Discuss with the students how it would be different to prepare the meal if they had only the tools available to prehistoric people. (Note: Make certain that collecting areas have not been sprayed with chemical pesticides! Some plants like milkweed can be poisonous unless processed correctly, and many mushrooms are poisonous regardless of how they are prepared. Consult field guides to edible plants and mushrooms and take appropriate precautions.)
2. Discuss with students the seasonal changes in food resources. What foods do we eat that are commonly seasonal? Examples: watermelon, cantaloupe, strawberries, blueberries, tomatoes, asparagus. In our culture, we can have rare seasonal foods all year around. Why?
3. Many food plants now eaten worldwide first originated in North and South America, such as corn, squash, pumpkins, potatoes, peppers, tomatoes, sunflowers, Jerusalem artichokes, almost all kinds of beans, chocolate, and tapioca (made from manioc). Discuss native American plants the Indians used which the Europeans did not have, such as corn or tobacco. How has the spread of these plants changed human history? Have students make posters showing how these native plants are used today. (Posters showing American Indian food and medicinal plants are available from the American Indian Program, National Museum of American History, Smithsonian Institution. See references.)

4. What can plants be used for besides food? Examples: musical instruments (gourds), medicines, dyes, polishing or scouring (horsetail rush), tipi or lodge poles, dressings for burns (cattail down), baskets, thatch, perfume or incense in religious rituals, soap (yucca root), torches (bundles of birch bark), and ropes (nettle fiber).

5. Discuss these questions with your students. How would your life be different if you had to survive on what you could find in your local area? What are some differences between the lives of people who farm and people who only hunt wild game and gather wild plants? Which would you rather do and why? What different kinds of problems would prehistoric farmers face than farmers face today?

Extensions

1. Have the students select one plant and observe its seasonal or life-cycle changes. Have each student become an expert on that plant, do library research on it, then present results to the class. Have them use field guides and keys for identification. What has the plant been used for? Where has the plant been found? What habitat? Is it native or introduced?

2. To give the students the idea of seasonal changes in resources, have them make four lists of the types of food they might have eaten during the different seasons. You might use four different groups for these and have the students discover that some resources would be unique to one season while other resources might be available through most of the year.

3. If spring, have the students plant a small garden. Have them use only tools that could be made from materials available to late prehistoric people such as the Oneota, Mill Creek, or Great Oasis cultures (stone, bone, wood, shell). Try using the tools in sod or open grassy areas, in the silt along a creek, or in a timbered area.

4. Make a list of some of our most commonly used modern farm plants, and research where they came from and which people originally used them. Set up a bulletin board with pictures of modern crops and their predecessors from the wild, as well as the American Indians who eat them today and have eaten them in the past. Today's "weeds" on chemical commercials such as lamb's-quarter and knotweed are actually nutritious plants that were cultivated and used as foods in prehistoric times.

W. Thomson '93

Birds in Prehistory

A great variety of birds have been identified in the faunal assemblages from Iowa archaeological sites. The archaeologists' interpretation of how these birds were used by Iowa's prehistoric inhabitants is based on ethnographic accounts and archaeological evidence. Birds were used for food, colorful feathers, artifacts, ornamentation, ceremonial paraphernalia, medicine bundles, sacred animals, and symbolic designs. Ethnographically, raptorial birds (hawks, eagles, and falcons) played an important role in the ceremonial life of many Plains Indian groups. Some groups reportedly kept birds of prey as pets or for their feathers. Fans made from raptors' wings were often used in dances and ceremonies. Some groups prized the feet of raptors for ceremonial ornaments.

We know from ethnographic accounts of groups such as the Osage, Omaha, and Arikara that medicine bundles composed of bird skin wrappings filled with sacred objects were used on ceremonial occasions. Stuffed bird skins also served as personal fetishes believed to bring good luck to their owners. In order to give some form to the bundle, the skull and bones of the wing and feet would be left attached to the skin. Although we are not certain of the existence of these bird bundles in prehistoric times, the occurrence of bones from the feet, wing, and skull of a bird found together in an archaeological site strongly suggests their existence.

Other ceremonial or decorative items manufactured from birds, such as feather headdresses, fans made from wings, and bird-bone flutes and whistles are also indicated by archaeological findings. At the Brewster site in Cherokee County in northwest Iowa, the lower wing and foot bones of raptors were particularly abundant. This suggests that Mill Creek people were hunting or trapping birds not only for food but also the manufacture of decorative and ceremonial objects. At the Cherokee Sewer site in northwest Iowa, a bird bone flute was recovered from a cultural horizon that dates to approximately 6,000 years ago. It is believed to be one of the oldest musical instrument ever found in the United States.

Many animals had symbolic values in American Indian cultures. Birds, however, were especially important as reflected in the many bird motifs seen in designs on both prehistoric and historic artifacts. A bird's behavior traits or striking markings may have led to it being considered sacred by the members of a particular culture. The Cheyenne consider the magpie to be a sacred messenger to the high god because it comes near to human habitation and overhears their conversations. The weeping or forked eye motif is found on artifacts from sites in the southern part of the Mississippi River valley and is occasionally found on artifacts from Iowa. Some archaeologists see a similarity in this motif and facial markings on the peregrine falcon.

How a bird was used determines what elements will be found at a site. If a bird had been killed for food or for feathers, a random scattering of its bones could be expected at a site with no particular element being more numerous than any of the others. However, if particular portions of certain birds were preferred for artifacts or ceremonial paraphernalia, then a disproportionately high percentage of these elements would be present.

The work of identifying bird remains is difficult. An extensive comparative collection containing the skeletons of many different bird species is needed. Even with such an excellent collection, bird identification is complicated by the fact that different species have skeletal elements which look alike. For example, bones of many of the ducks, geese, and swans (Family Anatidae) are difficult to tell apart. The same is true for the hawks and eagles (Family Accipitridae) and the many perching birds (Order Passeriformes). The task of identification is further complicated by the often fragmentary nature of the bird bone remains. Here are some of the birds identified from Iowa archaeological sites:

common loon
pied-billed grebe
double-crested cormorant
American white pelican
great blue heron
American bittern
turkey vulture
osprey
bald eagle
northern harrier
sharp-shinned hawk
Cooper's hawk
northern goshawk
red-shouldered hawk
broad-winged hawk
Swainson's hawk
red-tailed hawk
rough-legged hawk
golden eagle

prairie falcon
trumpeter swan
snow goose
Canada goose
wood duck
blue-winged teal
American widgeon
gadwall
mallard
northern pintail
northern shoveler
canvasback
lesser scaup
ruddy duck
greater prairie chicken
sharp-tailed grouse
wild turkey
northern bobwhite
sandhill crane

American coot
long-billed curlew
American woodcock
passenger pigeon (extinct)
great horned owl
barred owl
belted kingfisher
northern flicker
red-headed woodpecker
red-bellied woodpecker
snow bunting
rose-breasted grosbeak
red-winged blackbird
common grackle
Brewer's blackbird
bobolink
American crow
common raven

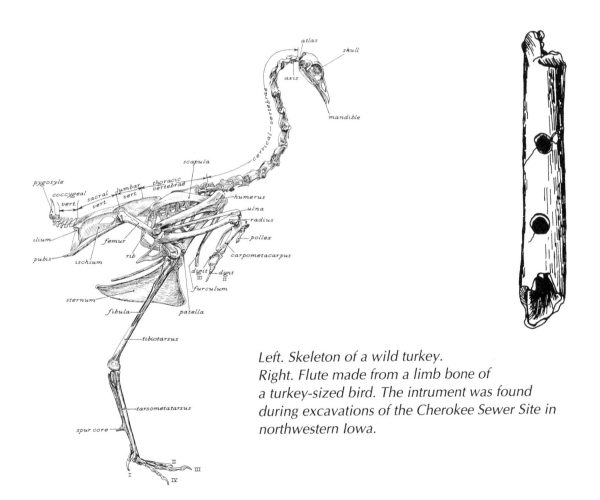

Left. Skeleton of a wild turkey.
Right. Flute made from a limb bone of
a turkey-sized bird. The intrument was found
during excavations of the Cherokee Sewer Site in
northwestern Iowa.

Activity 9. Bird Identification

Age Level   Grades 5–8

Time   1–2 hours

Focus

Students will become familiar with the processes of identification and interpretation of skeletal materials used by archaeologists.

Equipment

An articulated chicken or turkey skeleton obtained from a biology department or a nature center. (Alternately, a detailed bone identification guide might be used.) Dried individual bones from a chicken or turkey. Elmer's glue.

Activity Preparation

Process a chicken or turkey carcass by gently boiling the bones until all meat and gristle falls off easily. Rinse and dry the bones.

Activity

1. Introduce the students to the articulated skeleton or the detailed bone identification guide.
2. Have the students try to identify the individual bones you prepared by comparing them to the articulated skeleton. To simulate archaeological finds, do not give the students all the bones.
3. You may also want to break some of the bones. Make available all the pieces of a few of these bones, then see if the students can reconstruct the bones with glue.
4. For the rest of the broken bones, give the students only some of the fragments and ask them to identify the bone on the basis of a fragment.
5. The students should list which bones are present and which are missing and try to figure out why. A complete carcass or the bones found in the meatier portions might represent the remains of a meal. Only the bones from the wings might represent use in a ceremonial bundle. The longer, straighter bones may be missing—used for tools or ornamentation—and might be expected to be found elsewhere at a site in their altered state or maybe taken with the inhabitants when they moved to a different location.

Extensions

1. Discuss with the students which birds might be expected to be found in their local area. This could be based on personal experience or bird guides. Then take a trip to a natural area to try to view those expected bird species. Then discuss with your students the birds seen during the field trip and what those birds might have meant to prehistoric inhabitants of Iowa.
2. From a book on American Indian myths (see reference list for suggestions), read to the students some of the tales, legends, or myths in which birds or bird-like creatures are central characters. Or you can have students search the library for such stories. Discuss these myths with the students. Have students then choose an artistic format—play, reader's theater, artwork—to recreate images or events in the stories.

3. Have the students list birds that have been assigned symbolic meanings in our present day culture. You could collect photographs, sketches, and clippings ahead of time or assign students to do this as part of the activity. Discuss reasons why those particular birds may have been selected—overall appearance, specific attributes, behavior traits. Examples: bald eagle, a symbol of the United States; turkey, the traditional Thanksgiving main course; chicken, a derogatory challenge to someone; various birds as athletic symbols, e.g., St. Louis Cardinals, Seattle Seahawks, Atlanta Falcons, Detroit Redwings.

4. Have the students select a bird as a symbol for the class. Discuss why that bird was selected, what characteristics or behaviors may have influenced that choice. Using a symbolic representation of the selected bird, have the students incorporate that symbol into a logo, plaque, coat of arms, or other artistic rendition that could then be used for identifying the student or class. (Note the Office of the State Archaeologist "bird-man" logo on the back cover of this guide.)

5. Have the students make a bird feeding station that could be set up outside their school classroom or at home. Have the students record the species of birds that appear at different seasons. Have the students research migration flyways, note those in the local area, and look for certain birds during spring and fall migrations. Discuss the differences in what birds they observe seasonally and how seasonal variances could correlate with birds found at archaeological sites.

Archaeological Ethics and Law

Archaeology is the only science that destroys one of its principal objects of study. For this reason it is very important not to disturb a site unless you are trained in the methods of scientific excavation. Archaeologists do not dig just to find artifacts. They are really digging for information about the people of the past. Archaeologists try to discover who lived at a site, when, and their way of life. That is why archaeologists keep such careful records of what kinds of things are found together. Often they make a detailed map of where every artifact from a site was found, knowing this will give them more information about the activities of the people who once lived there.

By studying the past, we can learn many things which might help humanity now and in the future. For example, by studying the plants used as foods in prehistoric times, we can "rediscover" a forgotten native plant that could be cultivated and used as food for hungry people in the world today. Some plants that have been rediscovered and are now being researched by archaeologists are maygrass, knotweed, goosefoot, and marshelder.

By studying how cultures changed through time, archaeologists hope to understand what caused them to change. Some changes allowed a culture to flourish, grow, and extend its influence. Other changes might have had disastrous results. Archaeologists may be able to provide answers that could help us lessen the threat of war or learn to live with our environment.

Skeletons from ancient cemeteries contain information on diseases. Archaeologists and physical anthropologists are trying to find out which human diseases are due to diet, living conditions, climate, or heredity. For example, research being done today may someday help solve the mystery of arthritis.

Today there is a great danger that information about people of the past will be lost. Many archaeological sites that might have been able to tell us interesting things about ancient mammoth hunters, mound builders, or prehistoric villagers are being destroyed. The earliest American Indians hunted mammoths which became extinct. Archaeological sites are in danger of becoming extinct also. There are fewer and fewer of them every year. When animals are protected by law, they may avoid extinction. This is, of course, not true of sites. Archaeological sites are not renewable resources. When they are destroyed, they are gone forever.

Many things, even nature itself, can endanger sites. Much archaeological information is lost each year through erosion. Farmers plowing fields often cut into and destroy sites, breaking and scattering artifacts throughout the field. Urban development also poses a danger. Any building or excavation activities may destroy sites, and even if the artifacts are found later, most of the information about the lives of the prehistoric people will have been lost.

Another danger to archaeological sites is from people digging up artifacts without any regard for the site and the knowledge it contains. Archaeologists call this kind of excavation "pot-hunting." Sites are dug up, no records are kept, and the nicest artifacts are removed and put in cases. Displays of artifacts, no matter how beautiful they are, do not really tell us much about the lives of the people who made them. If we knew exactly where each artifact had been found, we would know something more about the people of the past. Pot-hunters thoughtlessly destroy any chance of learning much about the past.

Today people are aware that our supplies of natural resources like oil and coal are getting low. Many people know it is necessary to conserve the natural resources that are still left. Some people are learning that conservation of our cultural resources is also necessary if we want to increase our knowledge of the past. What are some examples of cultural resources and just how might the valuable information from them be conserved?

Cultural resources are historic or prehistoric sites with meaning to modern soeciety. Examples include places like Fort Atkinson in Winneshiek County. The fort, built in 1840 as an early U.S. Army post in the Iowa Territory, is now a state preserve. Old Capitol in Iowa City is another cultural resource—an important visual reminder of historic Iowa, informing people today a little more about Iowa's territorial past and early years of statehood. This building has been restored and is open to the public as a museum.

Archaeological sites are also cultural resources and important reminders of our past before there were any written records. Some of our archaeological sites have been protected as state preserves, like Malchow Mounds in Des Moines County, Turkey River Mounds in Clayton County, and Fish Farm Mounds in Allamakee County. A list of publicly owned archaeological sites, museums with archaeological displays, and resource centers devoted to Iowa Indians and prehistory is provided in Appendix B.

Today, it is against the law in Iowa to dig up and disturb any cemetery whether on public or private property. Iowa was the first state to pass a law specifically protecting unmarked, ancient burials and providing for the reburial of those remains already disinterred. Many states have since passed similar legislation in response to concerns expressed by modern American Indians for protection of their ancestors' cemeteries.

Where artifacts not associated with cemeteries have been found, individuals who own the land have to make personal decisions about whether to allow destruction of a site. They can help save a site by not disturbing the land in that area and by preventing digging for artifacts at the site. This protects the site for future generations.

It is sometimes impossible to protect every important archaeological site. For example, some sites are flooded by waters from reservoirs, and construction cannot always be stopped to save archaeological sites. What is being done about this problem? First, when they know an area is going to be disturbed, archaeologists like to make a very careful survey of the area. That way, even if the sites are destroyed, there will at least be a map showing where the sites were located and perhaps a collection of the artifacts found on the survey. Then if sites are discovered in an area that a reservoir will flood or a road will disturb, archaeologists can come in and excavate. They try to recover as much information as they can, because they know that the reservoir or road will destroy the site. They will probably never have a chance to return to the site to gather more data. Therefore, whenever possible, archaeologists prefer that the site be preserved and protected for future generations.

Some sites are restored, that is, rebuilt to look the same as they did in the past. Restoring sites is important to give everyone a chance to actually see how people lived in the past. That way the information is not only saved from being destroyed, but is presented in a way that gives everyone a better chance to learn about the past.

The most important protection an archaeological site and the information it provides can have is the interest of people—visiting sites, reading, talking to archaeologists. Many times the more people learn, the more interested they become. People who know something about the past are much less likely to destroy a site. They are also able to tell many others about the past and perhaps keep them from destroying sites. Educators play a very important role in preserving Iowa's past by making their students aware of these issues.

Anyone can be interested in archaeology and almost everyone is. Both amateur and professional archaeologistis have important roles. The difference between the professional and amateur archaeologist is that archaeology provides a living for the former while it remains primarily a hobby to the latter. To be well qualified, all archaeologists must acquire certain technical skills, theoretical knowledge, and powers of observation to conduct good field research and to competently analyze and interpret recovered materials. Most professionals have acquired a high degree of training and experience, primarily through formal education. This does not automatically make him or her competent, and certainly there are some amateur archaeologists who have more experience and are better trained than some professionals. At the same time, you would not choose someone to perform your appendectomy simply because they had read a few medical books and watched the surgery on television. For people truly concerned with finding out about the past, it is equally disheartening to witness a historic or prehistoric site being dug by individuals who have only read about excavation, visited museums, and mounted relic collections on their living room walls.

True amateur archaeologists, however, have an important role in Iowa archaeology. Thousands of square miles of land in Iowa have not been explored for archaeological sites. There are not enough professional archaeologists to learn everything there is to know about Iowa prehistory. Many times it has been the amateur archaeologists who have found sites with the most important new information about Iowa's early people.

Many amateur archaeologists in Iowa belong to the Iowa Archeological Society. Amateur archaeologists sometimes join with other amateur or professional archaeologists to carefully survey a much larger area. By working together in an organized group, they can learn more and share what they learn with each other. Whether amateur archaeologists look for artifacts by themselves or as a part of a group, they always carefully record every area where they find something. Amateur archaeologists know that even things like crude flakes of stone are important, because they represent the scraps of stone left behind by someone who was making a stone tool. The true amateur archaeologist is different from the casual person who just collects arrowheads. The amateur archaeologist records information and reports his or her finds to the proper authorities. Information collected but not shared quickly loses its value.

What would you or a student do if a site was found? A record of what was found and exactly where it was found should be sent to the Office of the State Archaeologist at The University of Iowa in Iowa City. The best way to know exactly where the site is located is to have an accurate map. In archaeology, it is important to always make sure you know your location. Archaeologists use U.S. Geological Survey topographic maps which are available for all parts of the state at a minimal cost from the Iowa Department of Natural Resources, Geological Survey Bureau, 109 Trowbridge Hall, Iowa City.

The Office of the State Archaeologist keeps a record of every site that is reported in the state. These records are kept on forms called site sheets. The site sheet contains important information describing the site—its location, who owns the land, and what kinds of things were found. A map of the site is drawn on the back of the site sheet. Occasionally pictures are drawn of any especially interesting artifacts found. These site sheets become a permanent record of your discovery.

At the Office of the State Archaeologist, the site will be given a site number and put on an official map. This way there is a record of all the sites in Iowa and a good source of information about just where early people lived throughout the state. This map also identifies areas where care should be taken to avoid destroying archaeological sites. If you or a student report a site, you would be sent a copy of the finished site sheet with an official number for the artifacts from the site. The artifacts from every Iowa site have their own numbers. That way people always know what site an artifact came from, even if artifacts from several sites would become mixed together. Professional archaeologists and the best amateur archaeologists number their artifacts in this way. These numbers are helpful to anyone who might later want to study the artifacts.

Actually learning to dig a site is another important part of archaeology. Excavations take time and careful planning that should be left to the professional archaeologists. Amateur archaeologists and students, however, can work on excavations through field schools sponsored by the Iowa

Archeological Society. Field schools are open to anyone who wants to learn to work on an excavation.

The most important thing about the field schools is that they are conducted by professional archaeologists. It is their experience and training that will insure the success of the project. The professional archaeologist does the more difficult measuring and recording as well as teaches the amateur archaeologists and students many things about the past. The professional archaeologist also has the responsibility of writing a scientific report telling what was learned at the project. At field schools, and at any archaeological excavation, crew members carefully wash and examine everything taken from the ground. All artifacts and even bones from archaeological excavations are given numbers as they are identified. This cataloging is another archaeological method you could learn at a field school.

In school, students may learn by practicing on a simulated dig. Students can enjoy talking about the things they have excavated and trying to interpret what they might mean. This is the same kind of thing that is done on a real excavation, as archaeologists get together to interpret their finds.

The Iowa Archeological Society publishes a *Newsletter* with stories or pictures of artifacts people have found throughout the state. This may help you as an educator identify some of the artifacts you or your students find. Longer and more detailed articles are found in the magazine-like *Journal of the Iowa Archeological Society*, which all members also receive. Each year the members of the Iowa Archeological Society hold spring and fall meetings. There, amateur and professional archaeologists share information about sites they have found or excavated. Some amateur archaeologists are given awards for the work they have done. The Iowa Archeological Society also awards amateurs that have become specially trained or certified in some of the methods of archaeology. Local chapters of the Society meet in several cities and towns. Membership in the Society is open to everyone interested in archaeology, including students. A copy of the membership form is provided at the end of this book. Sample copies of the IAS *Newsletter* are available upon request from the Office of the State Archaeologist.

Archaeology is hard work, demanding a lot of time, study, and often sore muscles. But archaeology is also fun—fun for learning and fun for doing for all ages. Here are some dos and don'ts for archaeology (emphasize these points to your students):

1. Do not be a "pot hunter," a person who ruins an artifact or a prehistoric site by careless digging. A pot hunter can do more damage than a bulldozer! An excavation is a very delicate operation. Each trowel full of earth must be checked carefully.

2. If you find something you think might be important, report your discovery at once to the Office of the State Archaeologist, the State Historical Society of Iowa, local county historical society, or the archaeology department of a university.

3. Do not "advertise" your find to people you cannot trust.

4. Refuse to buy or sell prehistoric artifacts; marketing encourages site destruction and manufacture of fakes.

5. Notify the Office of the State Archaeologist immediately if you know of a site that is going to be destroyed.

6. If you have a collection, be sure it is properly identified and recorded so it is of informational value 50 or 100 years from now.

Activity 10. Archaeology and You

Age Level   Grades 5–8

Time   1–1½ hours.

Focus

The student will become aware of some of the problems facing archaeology today and what they could do to help preserve archaeological resources.

Activity Preparation

Discuss the information in the background with the students or reproduce it in whole or in part for distribution prior to discussion.

Activity

Set up role-playing situations where:

1. A group of people must decide how to handle an archaeological site that is endangered by a construction project. Someone would represent each of these groups: landowners, professional archaeologists, amateur archaeologists, construction workers, politicians, people who want to buy houses that will be built there.
2. Hypothetical situation: A large, famous museum from Country X collected artifacts from a small, undeveloped country, Country Y, a hundred years ago without the knowledge or permission of tribal leaders. These artifacts have been on display at the museum in Country X since that time. Now, the current leaders of the small Country Y want these artifacts returned to them claiming the artifacts are an important part of that country's cultural and religious heritage and rightfully belong to them. Should the museum be forced to return these items? Who really "owns" these artifacts? Does the museum have a responsibility to keep the artifacts so a greater number of people can see them, enjoy them, learn from them? Does the museum have a responsibility to return something that may have originally been obtained unethically? Does the museum have a responsibility to return the artifacts simply because of the cultural association between these items and the living people of this culture and their claim of cultural and religious significance? What if the tribal leaders of Country Y a hundred years ago had full knowledge and had given their permission for the museum to collect and remove these artifacts?

(This situation is very relevant to what is occurring nationwide and worldwide. Recent federal legislation requires all U.S. museums and other institutions receiving federal funds to compile an inventory of human skeletal remains, associated funerary objects, unassociated funerary objects, and objects of cultural patrimony [having tribal ceremonial or religious significance]. All of the above items that can be affiliated with a specific tribe must be repatriated [returned] to that tribe upon tribal request. For more information on this legislation, and the issues involved, see Material Available from The American Indian Program in the References section which follows.)

Extension

Obtain sample site record sheets by writing to the Office of the State Archaeologist (OSA). The OSA will also send you information on how to fill out the sheets. Then make a copy for each student or group of students. Have each student or group select some location where evidence of some modern human activity has been left. Each student should then fill out a site sheet giving the information that might be useful to an archaeologist. Have each student try to locate one of his or her classmate's sites using the site record sheet. (This activity could also be used with Activity 3, "Picnic Ground Archaeology.")

Glossary

Absolute dating A method which assigns dates in calendar years.

Artifact Anything made or used by people. Projectile points, pottery sherds, and bone tools are examples of artifacts.

Context Relationship of the material remains in time and space.

Ecofacts Items left at a site which are not artifacts. Ecofacts may include both organic and inorganic materials. Seeds, snail shells, and wood charcoal are examples of ecofacts.

Ethnographic account A written or oral record of the lifeways of a particular people.

Excavation The process of uncovering archaeological deposits by digging.

Feature Nonportable artifacts which indicate human activity at a location. Burial mounds, cache pits, hearths, and post molds are examples of features.

Fish weir In streams or rivers, a sieve-like structure made of sticks with a rock foundation which would trap the fish but allow the water to continue flowing.

Flotation Separating small objects out of dirt by mixing the dirt with water, letting the lightest objects float to the surface, and collecting them in a fine screen.

Geology The study of the earth and the rocks of which it is composed.

Grid A group of small squares, all the same size, which are used to note the location of anything found on a site.

Historical archaeologist Scientist who studies societies for which there are written records.

Law of association The principle that an artifact is contemporary with the other objects in the same archaeological level or horizon.

Law of superposition The principle that objects or material buried or deposited earliest will be found deepest in the ground and those buried latest will be found on top.

Paleontology The study of plant and animal fossil remains.

Post mold Dark area of soil that shows where a post might once have been.

Prehistoric archaeologist A scientist who studies preliterate cultures, those which left no written records.

Pottery Anything made of clay which has been put in a fire to harden or strengthen it.

Relative dating Arranging materials in sequence, older or younger.

Seriation A system of dating artifacts based on the assumption that the popular use of certain artifact types goes through a period of rising popularity, reaches a peak, and finally declines in popularity.

Sherd Broken piece of pottery.

Site Any place with evidence of human activity.

Site number A distinct number given each archaeological site. Each site number consists of three parts: a numerical state designation (Iowa's is 13), a standard county abbreviation, and a unique number for each site within that county. For example, 13LA1 was the first site recorded in Louisa County, Iowa.

Stratification The layering of archaeological deposits in the ground.

Stratigraphy The inferred sequence of events at a site based on stratification.

Surface collection Recovery of archaeological material from the surface of the ground, with no excavation.

Survey Examine an area carefully to see if there is any evidence of archaeological sites.

Symbol Something used for or regarded as representing something else. A material object may often represent something immaterial, such as a belief.

Temper Nonplastic material, such as sand or ground shell, added to the clay to counteract shrinkage and facilitate uniform drying.

References

Unless indicated, the following sources are in print. Out-of-print sources often can be obtained through a local Area Education Agency or your public library.

Iowa Archaeology

Alex, Lynn Marie
1976 *Educational Series* 1–7. Office of the State Archaeologist, University of Iowa, Iowa City. (no charge)
1980 *Exploring Iowa's Past: A Guide to Prehistoric Archaeology.* University of Iowa Press, Iowa City. (out of print)
Anderson, Duane C.
1975 *Western Iowa Prehistory.* Iowa State University Press, Ames. (out of print)
1981 *Eastern Iowa Prehistory.* Iowa State University Press, Ames. (out of print)
Collins, James M.
1991 *The Iowa River Greenbelt: An Archaeological Landscape.* Special Publication. Office of the State Archaeologist, Iowa City.
Cooper, Tom C. (editor)
1982 *Iowa's Natural Heritage.* Iowa Natural Heritage Foundation and the Iowa Academy of Science, Des Moines.
McKusick, Marshall
1964 *Men of Anicent Iowa.* Iowa State University Press, Ames. (out of print)
1991 *The Davenport Conspiracy Revisited.* Iowa State Univeristy Press, Ames.
Morrow, Toby
1984 *Iowa Projectile Points.* Special Publication. Office of the State Archaeologist, Iowa City.
Vogel, Virgil J.
1983 *Iowa Place Names of Indian Origin.* University of Iowa Press, Iowa City.

Archaeology for Teachers

Ashmore, Wendy, and Robert J. Sharer
1988 *Discovering the Past: A Brief Introduction to Archaeology.* Mayfied, Mountain View, California.
Dyer, James
1983 *Teaching Archaeology in Schools.* Shire, Aylesbury, Buckinghamshire, United Kingdom.

Fagan, Brian M
1987 *The Great Journey: The Peopling of Ancient America.* Thames and Hudson, London.
1990 *Archaeology: A Brief Introduction.* 4th ed. Little, Brown, Boston.
1992 *People of the Earth. An Introduction to World Prehistory.* 7th ed. Harper Collins, New York.
Feder, Kenneth
1990 *Frauds, Myths, and Mysteries: Science and Pseudoscience in Archaeology.* Mayfield, Montain View, California.
Jennings, Jesse D.
1989 *Prehistory of North America.* 3rd ed. Mayfield, Mountain View, California.
Jennings, Jesse D. (editor)
1983 *Ancient North Americans.* W. H. Freeman, San Francisco.
Joukowsky, Martha
1980 *A Complete Manual of Field Archaeology: Tools and Techniques of Field Work for Archaeologists.* Prentice-Hall, Englewood Cliffs, New Jersey.
McMillon, Bill
1991 *The Archaeology Handbook: A Field Manual and Resource Guide.* John Wiley, New York.
Willey, Gordon R., and Jeremy A. Sabloff
1980 *A History of American Archaeology.* 2nd ed. W. H. Freeman, San Francisco.

Related Topics for Teachers

Berglund, Berndt, and Clare E. Boisby
1971 *The Edible Wild: A Complete Cookbook and Guide to Edible Wild Plants in Canada and North America.* Scribner, New York. (out of print)
Blaine, Martha R.
1979 *The Ioway Indians.* University of Oklahoma Press. Norman. (out of print)
Bowers, Alfred W.
1991 *Mandan Social and Ceremonial Organization.* Reprinted. University of Idaho Press, Moscow. Originally published 1950, University of Chicago Press, Chicago.

Densmore, Frances
1974 *How Indians Use Wild Plants for Food, Medicine and Crafts.* Dover Books, New York.
Elias, Thomas S., and Peter A. Dykeman
1990 *Edible Wild Plants: A North American Field Guide.* Sterling, New York.
Fletcher, Alice C., and Francis La Flesche
1992 *The Omaha Tribe.* Reprinted. 2 vols. University of Nebraska Press, Lincoln. Originally published 1911, Twenty-seventh Annual Report of the Bureau of American Ethnology, Smithsonian Institution, Washington, D.C.
Gibbons, Euell
1988 *Stalking the Wild Asparagus.* Reprinted. A. C. Hood, Brattleboro, Vermont. Originally published 1962, D. McKay, New York.
Gilmore, Melvin R.
1991 *Uses of Plants by the Indians of the Missouri River Region.* Reprinted. Enlarged ed. University of Nebraska Press, Lincoln. Originally published 1919, Thirty-third Annual Report of the Bureau of American Ethnology, Smithsonian Institution, Washington, D.C.
Hall, Alan
1990 *The Wild Food Trailguide.* Reprinted. Henry Holt, New York. Originally published 1976, Holt, Rinehart and Winston, New York.
Huffman, Donald M., Lois H. Tiffany, and George Knaphus
1989 *Mushrooms and Other Fungi of the Midcontinental United States.* Iowa State University Press, Ames. (out of print)
Peterson, Lee A.
1982 *A Field Guide to Eastern Edible Wild Plants.* Houghton Mifflin, Boston.
Yanovsky, Elias
1980 *Food Plants of the North American Indians.* Reprinted. Gordon Press, New York. Originally published 1936, Miscellaneous Publication 237, U.S. Department of Agriculture, Washington, D.C.

Archaeology for Students

Anderson, Joan
1988 *From Map to Museum: Uncovering Mysteries of the Past.* William Morrow, Morrow Junior Books, New York.

Baldwin, Gordon C.
1967 *Calendars to the Past: How Science Dates Archaeological Ruins.* Norton, New York. (out of print)
Branigan, Keith
1986 *Prehistory.* F. Watts, New York.
Brennan, Louis A.
1964 *The Buried Treasure of Archaeology.* Random House, New York. (out of print)
1973 *Beginners Guide to Archaeology.* Stackpole Books, Harrisburg, Pennsylvania. (out of print)
Chisholm, Jane
1982 *Living in Prehistoric Times.* EDC (Usborne), Tulsa. (out of print)
Cork, Barbara
1985 *Archaeology.* EDC (Usborne), Tulsa.
Cork, Barbara, and Struan Reid
1987 *The Young Scientist Book of Archaeology: Discovering the Past with Science and Technology.* EDC (Usborne), Tulsa. (out of print)
Coy, Harold
1973 *Man Comes to America.* Little, Brown, Boston. (out of print)
Folsom, Franklin and Mary Elting Folsom
1983 *America's Ancient Treasures.* 3rd ed. University of New Mexico Press, Albuquerque. (out of print)
Fradin, Dennis B.
1983 *Archaeology.* Children's Press, New York.
Gallant, Roy
1989 *Ancient Indians: The First Americans.* Enslow, Hillside, New Jersey.
Glubok, Shirley
1964 *The Art of North American Indians.* Macmillan, New York. (out of print)
1971 *The Art of the Southwestern Indians.* Macmillan, New York. (out of print)
1975b *The Art of Plains Indians.* Macmillan, New York. (out of print)
1976 *The Art of Woodland Indians.* Macmillan, New York. (out of print)
1978 *The Art of the Southeastern Indians.* Macmillan, New York. (out of print)
Grimm, William C.
1973 *Indian Harvests.* McGraw-Hill, New York. (out of print)
Johnson, Eileen (editor)
1990 *An Ancient Watering Hole: The Lubbock Lake Landmark Story.* Texas Tech University Press, Lubbock.

Johnson, Elden
  1988 *The Prehistoric Peoples of North America.*
        Minnesota Historical Society, St. Paul. (out
        of print)
Lattimore, Deborah
  1986 *Digging into the Past.* Educational Insights,
        Dominguez Hills, California.
Leroi-Gourhan, Andre
  1989 *The Hunters of Prehistory.* Macmillan Child
        Group, New York.
Lyttle, Richard B.
  1980 *People of the Dawn.* Atheneum, New York.
        (out of print)
Marston, Elsa
  1986 *Mysteries in American Archaeology.* Walker,
        New York.
McCord, Anne
  1977 *Early Man: The Story of the First People on
        Earth.* EDC (Usborne), Tulsa.
Merriman, Nick
  1989 *Early Humans.* Random House, Knopf Books
        for Young Readers, New York.
Morrison, Velma Ford
  1981 *Going on a Dig.* Dodd, Mead, New York.
        (out of print)
National Geographic Society
  1976 *Clues to America's Past.* National Geo-
        graphic Society, Washington, D.C. (out of
        print)
Nichols, Peter, and Belia Nichols
  1988 *Archaeology: The Study of the Past.* Eakin-
        Sunbelt, Austin.
Pickering, Robert B.
  1987 *I Can Be an Archaeologist.* Children's Press,
        Chicago.
Place, Robin
  1986 *Search for the Past.* Wright Group, Bothell,
        Washington. (out of print)
Raintree Publishers Staff
  1988 *Archaeology.* Raintree Stech-Vaughn, Mil-
        waukee.
Silverberg, Robert
  1986 *The Moundbuilders.* Ohio University Press,
        Athens.
Snow, Dean R.
  1989 *The Archaeology of North America.* Chelsea
        House, New York.
Snyder, Thomas F.
  1982 *Archeology Search Book.* McGraw, New
        York.
Stuart, Gene S.
  1979 *Secrets from the Past.* National Geographic,
        Washington, D.C.

Time-Life Books Editors
  1992 *The First Americans.* Time-Life Books, Alex-
        andria, Virginia.
Wheat, Pam, and Brenda Wharton
  1990 *Clues from the Past: A Resource Book on
        Archaeology.* Hendrick-Long, Dallas.
Wong, Ovid K.
  1988 *Prehistoric People.* Children's Press, Chi-
        cago.
Wood, Marian
  1990 *Ancient America.* Facts on File, New York.

Fiction Books for Students

Davis, Emmett
  1983 *Clues in the Desert.* Raintree Steck-Vaughn,
        Milwaukee.
Griffin, Peni
  1991 *A Dig in Time.* Macmillan, New York.
Hillerman, Tony
  1990 *A Thief of Time.* Reprinted. Paperback ed.
        Harper Collins, New York. Originally pub-
        lished 1988, Harper and Row, New York.
James, Carollyn
  1990 *Digging Up the Past: The Story of an Ar-
        chaeological Adventure.* F. Watts, New York.
Macaulay, David
  1979 *Motel of the Mysteries.* Houghton Mifflin,
        Boston.
Searcy, Margaret Zehmer
  1989 *Ikwa of the Mound-Builder Indians.* Peli-
        can, Gretna, Louisiana.
  1990 *The Charm of the Bear Claw Necklace.*
        Pelican, Gretna, Louisiana.
Trimble, Stephen
  1990 *The Village of the Blue Stone.* Macmillan
        Child Group, New York.

Teaching Materials, Curriculum Guides, Activities

Calduto, Michael J., and Joseph Bruchac
  1989 *Keepers of the Earth: Native American Sto-
        ries and Environmental Activities for Chil-
        dren.* Fulcrum, Golden, Colorado.
  1991 *Keepers of the Animals: Native American
        Stories and Wildlife Activities for Children.*
        Fulcrum, Golden, Colorado.
Cultural Heritage Education Team
  1993 *Intrigue of the Past, Investigating Archaeol-
        ogy.* Cultural Heritage Education Team,
        Anasazi Heritage Center, 27501 Highway
        91, Delores, Colorado 81323. (303) 882-
        4811.

Gilbert, B. Miles, Larry D. Martin, and Howard G. Savage
  1981 *Avian Osteology.* Modern Printing, Laramie, Wyoming.
Harrison, Michael
  1984 *Archaeology: Walney.* Museum Education Coordinator, Fairfax County Park Authority, 3701 Pender Drive, Fairfax, Virginia 22030 (no charge)
Hawkins, Nancy
  1984 *Classroom Archaeology.* Division of Archaeology, Office of Cultural Development, State of Louisiana, P.O. Box 44247, Baton Rouge, Louisiana 70804.
Hoyer, Julianne L.
  1979 *Teacher's Guide to Iowa Prehistory.* 3rd ed. Iowa's P.A.S.T., Office of the State Archaeologist, Iowa City.
Interaction Publishers, Inc.
  1982 *Dig 2.* Interaction Publishers, Inc. DBA Interact, Box 997, Lakeside, California 92040.
McNutt, Nan
  1988 *Project Archeology: Saving Traditions.* Sopris West, Inc., 1120 Delaware Avenue, Longmont, Colorado 80501. (For middle school and gifted elementary; a four month curriculum program).
Olsen, Stanley J.
  1979 *Osteology for the Archaeologist.* Papers of the Peabody Museum of Archaeology and Ethnology, Vol. 56, Nos. 3, 4, 5. Peabody Museum, Harvard University, Cambridge. (No. 3, The American Mastodon and the Woolly Mammoth; No. 4, North American Birds: Skulls and Mandibles; No. 5, North American Birds: Postcranial Skeletons). (out of print)
Oxendine, Joseph B.
  1988 *American Indian Sports Heritage.* Human Kinetics Books, Champaign, Illinois.
Pena, Elizabeth S.
  1989 *Archaeology Activity Pack.* New York State Bureau of Historic Sites, Peebles Island, Waterford, New York 12188. (no charge)
Price, T. Douglas, and Ann Birgitte Gebauer
  1989 *Adventures in Fugawiland: A Computer Simulation in Archaeology.* Mayfield, Mountain View, California.
Roller, Lib
  1981 *Indians of Tennessee: An Activity Manual.* Outdoor Education Department, Nashville Metro Schools, Nashville.

Sanders, Karen K.
  1986 *Archaeology Is More Than A Dig.* Tucson Unified School District, P.O. Box 40400, Tucson, Arizona 85717.
Smith, K. C., and Francis P. McManamon
  1991 *Archeology and Education: The Classroom and Beyond.* Archaeological Assistance Study, No. 2. National Park Service, U.S. Department of Interior, Washington, D.C.
Soffolk County Archaeological Association
  n.d. *Native Life and Archaeology Workbook.* Suffolk County Archaeological Association, P.O. Drawer AR, Stony Brook, New York 11790.

American Indian Mythology

Leland, Charles G.
  1992 *The Algonquin Legends of New England.* Dover, New York.
Lummis, Charles F.
  1992 *Pueblo Indian Folk-Stories.* University of Nebraska Press, Lincoln.
McLaughlin, Marie L.
  1990 *Myths and Legends of the Sioux.* University of Nebraska Press, Lincoln.
Neihardt, John G.
  1988 *Indian Tales and Others.* Reprinted. University of Nebraska Press, Lincoln. Originally published 1926, Macmillan, New York.
Newcomb, Franc J.
  1991 *Navaho Folk Tales.* University of New Mexico Press, Albuquerque.
Rachlin, Carol K., and Alice Marriott
  1977 *Plains Indian Mythology.* Penguin Books, Nal-Dutton, New York.

Magazines and Journals

AnthroNotes. Office of Public Information, Department of Anthropology, Smithsonian Institution, Washington, D.C. (no charge)
Archaeology. The Archaeological Institute of America, 135 William Street, New York, New York 10038.
Archaeology and Education. Archaeological Resource Centre, c/o Danforth Technical School, 840 Greenwood Avenue, Toronto, Ontario. (bi-annual newsletter)
Goldfinch, Iowa History for Young People. State Historical Society of Iowa, 402 Iowa Avenue, Iowa City, Iowa 52240. (see especially Volume 7, Number 1, 1985)

Journal of the Iowa Archeolgical Society. Office of the State Archaeologist, The University of Iowa, Iowa City, Iowa 52242.

National Geographic. National Geographic Society, Washington, D.C. 20013.

Smithsonian. Smithsonian Associates, 900 Jefferson Drive, Washington, D.C. 20560.

Special Features in Magazines

Lord, Lewis, with Sarah Burke
    1991 America Before Columbus. *U.S. News and World Report* 8 July:22–37.
National Geographic
    1991 1491: America before Columbus. October: 1–99.
MacLeish, William H.
    1991 1492 America: The Land Columbus Never Saw. *Smithsonian* November:34–52.
Newsweek
    1991 1492–1992. When Worlds Collide: How Columbus's Voyages Transformed Both East and West. Fall/Winter, Columbus Special Issue.
Rathje, William L.
    1991 Once and Future Landfills. *National Geographic* May:42–61
    1989 Rubbish! *The Atlantic* December:99–109

Articles in Journals

Moore, John H.
    1986 The Ornithology of Cheyenne Religionists. *Plains Anthropologist* 31:177–192.
O'Shea, John M., George D. Schrimper, and John K. Ludwickson
    1982 Ivory-Billed Woodpeckers at the Big Village of the Omaha. *Plains Anthropologist* 27:245–248.
Scott, Donna H.
    1979 Analysis of Avifauna from Five Sites in Northwest Iowa. *Journal of the Iowa Archeological Society* 26:43–79.
Smith, Bruce D.
    1989 Origins of Agriculture in Eastern North America. *Science* 246:1566–1571.

Materials Available from the American Indian Program*

Printed Materials

Green, Rayna, and Lisa Thompson (compilers)
    1992 *American Indian Sacred Objects, Skeletal Remains, Repatriation and Reburial: A Resource Guide.* Update to 1990 Guide. (no charge)
Green, Rayna, and Nancy M. Mitchell (compilers)
    1990 *American Indian Sacred Objects, Skeletal Remains, Repatriation and Reburial: A Resource Guide.* (no charge)
Green, Rayna, and J. Vigil
    1990 Issues in Contemporary American Indian Art: A Report on a Symposium. Jointly issued in *ATLATL: Native Arts Network: A Special Report.* (no charge)
Green, Rayna, and K. Stallard
    1991 *The Killing of the Waters: Dams, Development and American Indians.* (no charge)

Recorded Materials

Radio Smithsonian and the American Indian Program. An Audio Series on American Indians. Four 90 minute cassettes. *Living the Sky: American Indian Scientific Knowledge; The Only Good Indian: Images of American Indians; Glad Columbus Wasn't Looking for Turkey: American Indian History; Singing for Power: American Indian Art and Music.* Available for loan and no-cost copying.

Visual Materials

"Life in America After the Revolution: The Seneca Nation." A slide/audiotape presentation with teacher's manual. Available for loan and no-cost copying.
American Indian Food Plants. American Indian Medicinal Plants. African-American Food and Medicinal Plants. A poster series with a teacher's manual. Available for $6.00 per poster. Manual, no charge.

*Room 5119, National Museum of American History, Smithsonian Institution, Washington, D.C. 20560

Appendix A
A Brief Culture History of Iowa

by

Shirley J Schermer, William Green, and James M. Collins

Paleo-Indian

The *Paleo-Indian* period in North America dates to about 9,500–7,500 B.C. Paleo-Indians in Iowa encountered vastly different environments than those of the recent past. The climate was cooler and wetter than present averages. In north central Iowa, Paleo-Indians lived in recently deglaciated landscapes covered by boreal and conifer-hardwood forests, shifting through time to elm- and oak-dominated woodlands. Woodlands predominated in most of the state as well, and prairie, if present, was very limited.

The Clovis complex is the earliest well defined archaeological culture currently known in North America. Clovis and other fluted projectile point styles were made during the first two-thirds of the Paleo-Indian period, and Dalton and unfluted point forms date to the latter one-third of the period. Aside from these lanceolate (lance-shaped) points, defining characteristics of the Paleo-Indian period include distinctive butchering tools, extensive use of exotic chert types, and specialized lithic technologies. Fluted and unfluted point forms have been recovered as surface finds from upland and valley locations throughout Iowa.

Paleo-Indian peoples were extremely mobile, hunting various animals including now-extinct large mammals such as mammoth, mastodon, and giant bison. Most Paleo-Indian sites so far located in the United States are large mammal kill sites, and little is known of other site types. No Paleo-Indian base camps have yet been documented in Iowa. To date, the best documented fluted point site in Iowa is a plow-disturbed cache of Clovis points known as the Rummells-Maske site in Cedar County.

Archaic

The *Early Archaic* period (7,500–5,500 B.C.) is viewed as a somewhat transitional period between cultures relying on big game for subsistence and those with a more rounded forager adaptation. Environments changed relatively quickly, as deciduous woodlands, mixed with prairies in western areas, became established over most of the state. Populations probably depended on bison in western Iowa and on deer and elk in eastern Iowa. These large mammals were supplemented by smaller game and by increasing use of plant foods. Settlement types included somewhat permanent base camps and seasonally occupied resource procurement camps. Excavated sites, such as the Cherokee Sewer site, suggest local populations were small and that they were tied to a seasonal round of resource exploitation. Representative artifacts include medium to large spear points, often with serrated and beveled blade edges.

The *Middle Archaic* period (5,500–2,500 B.C.) is so poorly known in Iowa that it has normally been lumped with the Early Archaic. Cultural adaptations may have been similar, but environmental conditions became increasingly arid throughout the period. The Middle Archaic period corresponds to the warmest and driest postglacial period, commonly referred to as the Atlantic episode, or the Hypsithermal. Human populations throughout the Midwest gravitated to the wetter river valleys, and because of this, Middle Archaic sites are often deeply buried and difficult to locate. During the Hypsithermal, great masses of silt filled river valleys, and alluvial fan development was rapid. Many Middle Archaic sites are buried in these alluvial sediments.

By the *Late Archaic* period (2,500–500 B.C.) the Midwest was becoming a fairly crowded place with the incidence of intergroup encounter rising sharply. This situation resulted in similar subsistence strategies over broad areas, but also in increased territoriality, local differentiation in artifact styles, and development of intergroup trading networks. The end of the dry Hypsithermal resulted in increased stability of the resource base and made many previously unsuitable areas attractive for settlement. Population levels appear to have increased substantially, and a somewhat sedentary lifeway as well as construction of large ossuaries (multiple-interment cemeteries) are documented for this period. The use of communal cemeteries reinforces the interpretation that populations were becoming more sedentary.

Woodland

The Woodland tradition (500 B.C.–A.D. 1000) was characterized by improved technologies, such as ceramic production and horticulture, leading to an overall increase in productive efficiency, and by the construction of burial mounds. Although these characteristics originated during the Archaic, only after 500 B.C. did they come together and become adopted over a wide area.

Woodland peoples refined their hunter-gatherer adaptations, making heavy use of fish and clams in major river valleys, and continuing to exploit deer and bison. Dependence on cultivated plants increased. Native plants often thought of as weeds today were grown for their nutritious seeds. Woodland farmers developed domesticated varieties of some of these native grain crops long before corn or beans became important. Climatic conditions approached modern averages, landform development stabilized in most places except in flood plains and stream channels, and vegetation patterns were much like the forest-prairie mix documented by nineteenth-century land surveys.

Early Woodland settlements (500–100 B.C.) in the Midwest were small and seasonally occupied. Early Woodland subsistence patterns in Iowa are not well known, but they probably involved broad-based procurement of mammals, birds, and aquatic species. Early Woodland peoples built large burial mounds similar to some in Ohio, and they interacted with groups throughout the Midwest, as evidenced by artifacts made of exotic raw materials. The typical Early Woodland spear point was a straight stemmed or contracting stemmed point, and pottery of the period includes both a thick, flat-bottomed type (500–300 B.C.) and a thinner, bag-shaped type often decorated with incised lines in geometric patterns (300–100 B.C.). Early Woodland sites are relatively common in the Mississippi Valley but are difficult to identify in central and western Iowa. Perhaps groups on the eastern Great Plains retained an Archaic lifestyle during this period.

The *Middle Woodland* period (100 B.C.–A.D. 300) is noted for its refined artworks, complex mortuary program, and extensive trade networks. Middle Woodland communities throughout the Midwest were linked by a network archaeologists refer to as the Hopewell Interaction Sphere. Trading involved materials such as Knife River flint from North Dakota and obsidian from the Yellowstone Park area. Also exchanged through the Hopewell network were artifacts of marine shell, copper, mica, and several pipestones, as well as high quality ceramic vessels and possibly perishable materials which have not survived archaeologically.

Elaboration of the mortuary program and social stratification indicate increased levels of social and political complexity. However, most Middle Woodland peoples probably lived in small communities or farmsteads, focusing their subsistence economy on food resources in large river valleys and tending gardens of squash, tobacco, and native grain crops such as marshelder and goosefoot. Typical Middle Woodland tools included broad, corner-notched spear points and finely made, thin blades.

By *Late Woodland* times (A.D. 300–1000) the continent-wide exchange of exotic goods declined but interaction between communities and tribes continued. Population levels apparently increased rapidly. In some parts of Iowa, Late Woodland peoples aggregated into large, planned villages, but in most of the state settlements continued to be small and generally became more dispersed across the landscape. Uplands and small interior valleys became settled or more heavily utilized. Late Woodland peoples introduced the bow and arrow into the Midwest. Continued native crop horticulture and diversified hunting and gathering provided the subsistence base through most of the period. Corn was introduced to many groups after around A.D. 800 but did not form a staple crop until the Late Prehistoric period.

Mound construction was generally simpler than in the Middle Woodland period, but regular aggregations for ritual and other purposes are probably reflected in the Late Woodland mound groups found throughout the state. Groups of linear, effigy, and conical mounds in northeastern Iowa form a distinctive element of the Effigy Mound Culture (A.D. 650–1000). The living sites of Effigy Mound peoples show a seasonal settlement pattern involving fish and shellfish collection during warm seasons in the main river valleys, nut harvesting in uplands in the fall, and winter use of rockshelters. Effigy Mound populations may have lived in dispersed groups in the interior of northeast Iowa during much of the year, coalescing regularly in the Mississippi valley to exploit the vast array of seasonally available resources. The effigy mound groups along the Mississippi bluff line may have signified the territories of loosely related nuclear or extended family units which met seasonally and merged into a larger social unit.

Late Prehistoric

The *Plains Village* pattern appeared in Late Prehistoric times (A.D. 1000–1650) marking the beginning of a distinctive adaptation to the tall grass prairie/short grass plains ecotone of South Dakota, Nebraska, western Iowa, and southern Minnesota. Improved corn varieties, garden surpluses, new storage methods, earthlodge houses, and a complex social organization were common to these Late Prehistoric villagers. Bison meat was a common item in the diet, and hides were processed for clothing, robes, and coverings for tipis and lodges. Bison bones were modified into a variety of tools such as scapula hoes, used in gardening and digging.

One of the earliest of the Plains Village cultures was *Great Oasis.* Great Oasis culture developed from the local Late Woodland culture around A.D. 1000. Great Oasis sites are found over a wide area in the eastern Great Plains. Villages were situated on low terraces above the flood plains of rivers and streams, and on lake shores. Large, permanent villages may have been occupied by the entire population throughout the fall, winter, and spring. Smaller, temporary campsites were used for seasonal procurement of resources. During the summer a communal bison hunt or the establishment of small campsites for horticultural purposes may have led to temporary abandonment of the large settlements.

Mill Creek, a northwest Iowa culture of this period, is part of what prehistorians refer to as the Initial variant of the Middle Missouri tradition. Mill Creek villages appear as deep midden deposits on terraces above the Big and Little Sioux rivers and their tributaries. Many of the well planned, compact villages were fortified with log palisades, and encircling ditches. Within the villages were individual earthlodges with large internal storage pits. Mill Creek people were semisedentary horticulturalists who grew a large amount of corn along with the native crops, possibly using ridged-field agriculture. It is likely that, as with other Plains Village groups, a communal bison hunt was conducted on one or more occasions during the year. Mill Creek people maintained connections, possibly through trade, with major prehistoric centers in the Mississippi valley, such as the famous site of Cahokia near St. Louis.

The *Central Plains* tradition consisted of cultures in Kansas, Nebraska, western Missouri, and southwestern Iowa. Many Central Plains sites were settled farming communities whose residents built substantial earthlodge houses. The archaeological remains of communities along the Missouri River in eastern Nebraska, southwestern Iowa, northwestern Missouri,

and northeastern Kansas are grouped into what is called the Nebraska phase. Any relationships between the prehistoric Nebraska phase and historic tribes are unclear, although the historic Pawnee may have roots in the Central Plains tradition.

Over 80 Central Plains earthlodges have been recorded in the Glenwood locality, Mills County. They represent a fully-developed expansion of Nebraska phase people into southwestern Iowa around A.D. 1050–1250. Glenwood settlements were individual farmsteads or small clusters of earthlodges dispersed along ridge summits, low terraces, and valley wall slopes in the Loess Hills and adjacent landforms.

During the Late Prehistoric period the *Oneota* culture dominated much of eastern Iowa as well as extensive parts of central and northwestern Iowa. Oneota peoples lived throughout the Midwest between around A.D. 1050 and 1700. Oneota villages were large and permanent or semipermanent. Houses varied in form from small, square or oval single-family dwellings to longhouses with many families. The subsistence economy was based on fishing, hunting, plant collecting, and agriculture. Distinct Oneota groups occupied widely separated regions of Iowa. Each group, or phase, occupied a core locality where villages were densely packed on the landscape. These core areas are surrounded by huge territories that were probably used for hunting, gathering, and other resource procurement. Although the various phases appear to have been generally autonomous, there was probably a great deal of interaction and socio-political cohesion among them. Oneota complexes are ancestral to several midwestern tribes such as the Iowa, Oto, Missouri, and Winnebago.

Historic Indians and Euro-Americans

Several Oneota sites in northeastern and northwestern Iowa bridge the prehistoric and historic eras (A.D. 1640–1700). Early French trade goods such as glass beads, finger rings, and gunflints are found at sites dominated by native-made material. In Iowa the term "protohistoric" denotes this period, when European goods were arriving and other influences were felt but before European peoples started to make extensive written records of the area.

Indian groups residing in or using portions of Iowa seasonally in protohistoric times included the Iowa, Oto, Omaha, perhaps the Missouri, and the Middle and Eastern Dakota. These groups were essentially sedentary, but elements of their populations made wide-ranging seasonal forays for hunting and warfare.

After around 1650, European competition for tribal

alliances and trade, and European diseases, drastically changed the structure of and relationships among Indian groups. Tribal population declined and white dispossession of traditional territories became common. In Iowa, the tribes mentioned above gave way to Great Lakes groups including the Sauk, Mesquakie (Fox), Winnebago, and Potawatomi. Perhaps the best known of these groups among Iowans is the Mesquakie.

The name Mesquakie means "people of the red earth." Oral history indicates a tribal origin in the lower Great Lakes. At the time of earliest French contact, the Mesquakies had recently moved from Michigan to Wisconsin. In the early 1700s French pressure forced the tribe into Illinois. By 1750, the Mesquakies considered Iowa their homeland, and they established priority rights to the Iowa River valley by 1800. Further pressured by white incursion into Iowa, the Mesquakies ceded Iowa lands in 1804, 1832, 1836, 1837, and 1842. Most Mesquakie people continued to live in villages in the Iowa River valley, moving farther up river with each land cession. Some Mesquakies remained in Iowa even after the "official" removal of Indians from Iowa in 1845. In the 1850s, the Mesquakies residing in Iowa and those returning from western reservations purchased land in Tama County, and the Mesquakie settlement was legally founded.

European-sponsored enterprises affecting Iowa in the early Historic period included the fur trade and, in northeastern Iowa, lead mining. In 1762, the area that is now Iowa came under Spanish rule. The Mines of Spain State Recreation Area, Dubuque County, is a portion of Julien Dubuque's original land grant which he received from the Spanish government in 1796. The Mesquakie Indians, who moved into the area in the mid-1770s, allowed Dubuque to mine for lead in what they considered their territory from 1788 to Dubuque's death in 1810. Two other Spanish land grants were given to private individuals—one to Basil Giard in what is now Clayton County and one to Louis Tesson in what is now Lee County. The United States obtained Iowa as part of the Louisiana Purchase in 1803, and soon thereafter President Jefferson sent Lewis and Clark to explore the Louisiana Purchase. They traveled up the Missouri River in 1804, meeting with the Oto and Missouri tribes and hunting in the Loess Hills. In 1809, Fort Madison was built, followed by Fort Armstrong at Rock Island, Fort Crawford at Prairie du Chien, and Fort Atkinson in Winneshiek County. In 1833, much of eastern Iowa was opened for non-Indian settlement and by 1850, small towns were scattered across the state. Early settlements were along rivers, especially in eastern Iowa. By 1870 railroads had spread across the state, and river transportation declined in importance.

Most of Iowa's cities and towns were established by the mid-1800s. Farms covered the state, and industries such as coal mining flourished. By the time of statehood in 1846, the character of modern Iowa had been formed by events of its most recent history.

References

General

Anderson, Duane C.
1975 The Development of Archaeology in Iowa: An Overview. *Proceedings of the Iowa Academy of Science* 82:71–86.
McKusick, Marshall (editor)
1971 *Prehistoric Investigations.* Report 3. Office of the State Archaeologist, Iowa City.

Paleo-Indian

Agogino, George A., and W. D. Frankforter
1960 A Paleo-Indian Bison Kill in Northwestern Iowa. *American Antiquity* 25:414–415.
Anderson, Adrian D., and Joseph A. Tiffany
1972 Rummels-Maske: A Clovis Find Spot in Iowa. *Plains Anthropologist* 17:55–59.
Frison, George C.
1991 *Prehistoric Hunters of the High Plains.* 2nd ed. Academic Press, San Diego.
Graham, Russell W.
1982 Clovis People in the Midwest: The Importance of the Kimmswick Site. *The Living Museum* 44(2):27–29.
Wheat, Joe Ben
1967 A Paleo-Indian Bison Kill. *Scientific American* January:44–52.

Archaic

Anderson, Duane C., and Holmes A. Semken, Jr. (editors)
1980 *The Cherokee Excavations: Holocene Ecology and Human Adaptations in Northwestern Iowa.* Academic Press, New York.
Anderson, Duane C., Michael Finnegan, John Hotopp, and Alton K. Fisher
1978 The Lewis Central School Site (13PW5): A Resolution of Ideological Conflicts at an Archaic Ossuary in Western Iowa. *Plains Anthropologist* 23:183–219.

46

Fisher, Alton K., W. D. Frankforter, Joseph A. Tiffany, Shirley J. Schermer, and Duane C. Anderson
 1985 Turin: A Middle Archaic Burial Site in Western Iowa. *Plains Anthropologist* 30:195–218.
Phillips, James L., and James A. Brown (editors)
 1983 *Archaic Hunters and Gatherers in the American Midwest.* Academic Press, New York.

Woodland

Benn, David W.
 1980 *Hadfield's Cave: A Perspective on Late Woodland Culture in Northeastern Iowa.* Report 13. Office of the State Archaeologist, Iowa City.
Benn, David W. (editor)
 1990 *Woodland Cultures on the Western Prairies: The Rainbow Site Investigations.* Report 18. Office of the State Archaeologist, Iowa City.
Brose, David S., and Nomi Greber (editors)
 1979 *Hopewell Archaeology: The Chillicothe Conference.* Kent State University Press, Kent, Ohio.
Farnsworth, Kenneth B., and Thomas E. Emerson (editors)
 1986 *Early Woodland Archaeology.* Center for American Archeology Press, Kampsville, Illinois.
Logan, Wilford D.
 1976 *Woodland Complexes in Northeastern Iowa.* Publications in Archaeology 15. National Park Service, U.S. Department of the Interior, Washington, D.C.
Mallam, R. Clark
 1976 *The Iowa Effigy Mound Manifestation: An Interpretive Model.* Report 9. Office of the State Archaeologist, Iowa City.
 1976 The Mound Builders: An American Myth. *Journal of the Iowa Archeological Society* 23:145–175.
 1984 Some Views on the Driftless Area in Iowa. *Proceedings of the Iowa Academy of Science* 91:16–21.
Theler, James L.
 1987 *Woodland Tradition Economic Strategies: Animal Resource Utilization in Southwestern Wisconsin and Northeastern Iowa.* Report 17. Office of the State Archaeologist, Iowa City.

Tiffany, Joseph A., Shirley J. Schermer, James L. Theler, Douglas W. Owsley, Duane C. Anderson, E. Arthur Bettis III, and Dean M. Thompson
 1988 The Hanging Valley Site (13HR28): A Stratified Woodland Burial Locale in Western Iowa. *Plains Anthropologist* 33:219–259.

Mill Creek and Great Oasis

Anderson, Duane C.
 1981 *Mill Creek Ceramics: The Complex from the Brewster Site.* Report 14. Office of the State Archaeologist, Iowa City.
 1987 Toward a Processual Understanding of the Initial Variant of the Middle Missouri Tradition: The Case of the Mill Creek Culture of Iowa. *American Antiquity* 52:522–537.
Dallman, John E.
 1983 *A Choice of Diet: Response to Climatic Change.* Report 16. Office of the State Archaeologist, Iowa City.
Tiffany, Joseph A.
 1982 *Chan-Ya-Ta: A Mill Creek Village.* Report 15. Office of the State Archaeologist, Iowa City.

Glenwood (Central Plains)

Anderson, Adrian D.
 1960 The Glenwood Sequence: A Local Sequence for a Series of Archaeological Manifestations in Mills County, Iowa. *Journal of the Iowa Archeological Society* 10(3).
Blakeslee, Donald J. (editor)
 1978 *The Central Plains Tradition: Internal Development and External Relationships.* Report 11. Office of the State Archaeologist, Iowa City.
Brown, Lionel
 1967 *Pony Creek Archaeology.* Publications in Salvage Archaeology No. 5. River Basin Surveys, Smithsonian Institution, Lincoln, Nebraska.
Gradwohl, David M.
 1969 *Prehistoric Villages in Eastern Nebraska.* Publications in Anthropology 4. Nebraska State Historical Society, Lincoln.
Green, William
 1991 The Paul Rowe Archaeological Collection: A Key to Central Plains Prehistory. *Plains Anthropologist* 36:79–85.

Green, William (editor)
1990 Glenwood Culture Paleoenvironment and Diet: Analysis of Plant and Animal Remains from the Wall Ridge Earthlodge (13ML176), Mills County, Iowa. *Research Papers* 15(6). Office of the State Archaeologist, Iowa City.

Zimmerman, Larry J.
1977 *Prehistoric Locational Behavior: A Computer Simulation.* Report 10. Office of the State Archaeologist, Iowa City.
1977 The Glenwood Local Sequence: A Reexamination. *Journal of the Iowa Archeological Society* 24:62–83.

Oneota and Ioway

Anderson, Duane C.
1973 Ioway Ethnohistory: A Review (Parts 1 and 2). *Annals of Iowa* 41:1228–1241, 42:41–59.

Harvey, Amy
1979 *Oneota Culture in Northwestern Iowa.* Report 12. Office of the State Archaeologist, Iowa City.

Henning, Dale R.
1970 Development and Interrelationship of Oneota Culture in the Lower Missouri River Valley. *Missouri Archaeologist* 32:1–180.

McKusick, Marshall
1973 *The Grant Oneota Village.* Report 4. Office of the State Archaeologist, Iowa City.

Mott, Mildred
1938 The Relation of Historic Indian Tribes to Archaeological Manifestations in Iowa. *Iowa Journal of History and Politics* 36:227–314.

Straffin, Dean F.
1971 *The Kingston Oneota Site.* Report 2. Office of the State Archaeologist, Iowa City.

Wedel, Mildred Mott
1959 Oneota Sites on the Upper Iowa River. *The Missouri Archaeologist* 21(2, 4).
1961 Indian Villages on the Upper Iowa River. *Palimpsest* 42:561–592.
1981 The Ioway, Oto, and Omaha Indians in 1700. *Journal of the Iowa Archeological Society* 28:1–13.

Appendix B
A Selected List of Archaeological Sites, Museums, and Resource Centers in Iowa

Archaeological Sites

Allamakee County

Effigy Mounds National Monument, 3 miles north of Marquette on Iowa 76. (319) 873-3491.

Fish Farm Indian Mounds State Preserve, 6 miles north of Lansing on Iowa 26.

Appanoose County

Honey Creek State Park, mounds, west of Moravia on Iowa 142. (515) 724-3739.

Calhoun County

Twin Lakes State Park, mounds, 7.5 miles north of Rockwell City, west side of North Twin Lake, on Iowa 124. (712) 657-2639.

Clayton County

Pike's Peak State Park, conical and effigy mounds, 1 miles south of McGregor on Iowa 340. (319) 873-2341.

Turkey River Mounds State Preserve, approximately 5.5 miles south of Guttenberg, east 1 mile on gravel road to parking lot. (319) 873-2341.

Des Moines County

Malchow Mounds State Preserve, approximately 1 miles north of Kingston on Iowa 99, parking lot on west side of highway.

Starr's Cave State Preserve, 3299 Irish Ridge Road, north edge of Burlington. (319) 753-5808.

Dubuque County

Four Mounds, approximately 2 miles north of the intersection of U.S. 52 and Peru Road, north edge of Dubuque; contact the Four Mounds Foundation for permission. (319) 557-7292.

Little Maquoketa River Mounds State Preserve, approximately 2 miles north of Dubuque city limits on U.S. 52 and Iowa 3, sign and parking lot on west side of road.

Mines of Spain, south of Dubuque on U.S. 52, look for sign to turn east on gravel road, a wide variety of prehistoric and historic site types; a visit to the E. B. Lyons Nature Center first for an overview is recommended. (319) 556-0620.

Iowa County

Indian Fish Trap State Preserve, from U.S. 6 and U.S. 151 in Homestead, go about 50 yards west to the parking area for the Amana Nature Trail. Follow the trail for about 2 miles to the site. Visible only during times of low water.

Jackson County

Bellevue State Park, mounds on bluff edge along trail. Park is located just south of Bellevue on U.S. 52. (319) 872-4019.

Louisa County

Toolesboro Mounds National Historic Landmark Site and State Preserve, 8 miles east of Wapello on Iowa 99.

Lee County

Old Fort Madison, in Fort Madison.

Linn County

Palisades Kepler State Park, mounds, west of Mt. Vernon on U.S. 30. (319) 895-6039.

Pleasant Creek State Park, mounds, 7 miles west of I-380 in Cedar Rapid on Blair's Ferry Road (E36), then right on W36 for 3.5 miles.

Lyon County

Blood Run National Historic Landmark Site, permission required for access; contact Lyon County Conservation Board. (712) 472-2217.

Mahaska County

Cedar Bluffs Natural Area, mound, rockshelters, archaeological remains of historic farmstead; contact County Conservation Board for information and directions. (515) 673-9327.

Warren County

Woodland Mounds State Preserve, from the intersection of highways 69 and 92 in Indianola, take 92 east about 4.5 miles to County S23 in Ackworth. Turn south and go about 1 mile, turn east and follow road about 2.5 miles to the preserve entrance north of the road. (515) 961-0439.

Hickory Hills County Park, approximately 11 miles south of Indianola on U.S. 69 near intersection with County Road G76. Mounds and historic farmstead site.

Webster County

Dolliver Memorial State Park, mounds, 3 miles northwest of Lehigh, Iowa 50. (515) 359-2539.

Winneshiek County
Fort Atkinson State Preserve, edge of town of Fort Atkinson, Iowa 24. (319) 425-4161.

Contact the Iowa Department of Natural Resources, Des Moines, for a directory to the State Preserves system. (515) 281-5145.

Museums with Archaeological Exhibits

Arnold's Park
Gardner Sharp Cabin. (712) 332-7248 or 337-3211.

Battle Creek
Battle Creek Museum of Natural History

Bellevue
Bellevue State Park, nature center has a small display. (319) 872-401.

Cedar Falls
University of Northern Iowa Museum, 3219 Hudson Road. (319) 273-2188.

Cherokee
Sanford Museum and Planetarium, 117 East Willow Street. (712) 225-3922.

Davenport
Putnam Museum, 1717 W. 12th Street. (319) 324-1933.

Decorah
Vesterheim Norwegian-American Museum, 502 West Water. (319) 382-9681.

Des Moines
State Historical Museum, 600 East Locust Street. (515) 281-5111.

Dubuque
E. B. Lyons Nature Center, Mines of Spain. (319) 556-0620.
Woodward Riverboat Museum, Ice Harbor. (319) 557-9545.

Effigy Mounds National Monument
Visitor's Center at the monument. (319) 873-3491.

Forest City
Timberland Museum, R. R. 2, Box 52. (515) 581-2992.

Glenwood
Mills County Historical Museum and nearby earthlodge reconstruction. (712) 527-9339.

Iowa City
The University of Iowa Museum of Natural History (Iowa Hall), Macbride Hall, The University of Iowa. (319) 335-0480.

Maquoketa
Sagers Museum, Maquoketa Caves State Park, 6 miles northwest of Maquoketa on Iowa 428. (319) 652-5833.

Rock Island, Illinois
Hauberg Indian Museum, 1510 46th Avenue.

Sioux City
Sioux City Public Museum, 2901 Jackson Street. (712) 279-6174.

Urbandale
Living History Farm, 1700 Ioway Indian Village, 2600 NW 111th Street. (515) 278-5286.

Waterloo
Grout Museum of History and Science, 503 South Street. (319) 234-6357.

A number of local and county historical museums and county conservation board nature centers also have archaeological exhibits. Check those in your community.

Resource Centers

American Indian Center, 619 6th Street, Sioux City 51105. (712) 255-8957.

American Indian Community Center, 1000 College, Des Moines 50314. (515) 243-1745.

American Indian Rights Organization, Iowa State University, Ames

American Indian Student Association Chicano-Native American Center, 308 Melrose Avenue, Iowa City 52240. (319) 335-8298.

Iowa Archeological Society, Jerry Phillips, President (contact Office of the State Archaeologist). (319) 335-2389.

Office of the State Archaeologist, Eastlawn, The University of Iowa, Iowa City 52242. (319) 335-2389.

Office of International Education and Services, International Center, The University of Iowa, Iowa City 52242. (319) 335-0335.

Quad City League of Native Americans, 418 19th Street, Rock Island, Illinois. (309) 793-6391. (Membership includes both the Iowa and Illinois sides of the Quad-Cities).

State Historical Society of Iowa, Capitol Complex, Des Moines 50319. (515) 281-5111.

United Native American Student Association, Iowa State University, Ames.

Appendix C
Bone Tools

by
*Toby Morrow**

Introduction

As a result of his hunting activities, prehistoric man had access to a variety of animal bones as a raw material for tools. Along with artifacts of stone, shell, and wood, bone implements became an important component of many primitive technologies. As a raw material, bone is tough and slightly brittle. Certain bones that make up the mammalian skeleton, such as that depicted for the bison below, were especially well suited for certain tool forms. With only slight modifications, the scapulae of bison and elk could be made into blades for hoes, and the ulnae of deer could be worked into awls. Other types of tools such as fishhooks required considerable labor to reach their desired form. The hardness and resilience of bone made it particularly useful for certain purposes. While softer than most stone and harder than wood, bone tools required special techniques of manufacture.

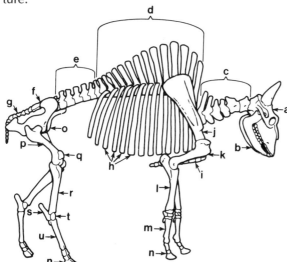

Generalized skeleton of the bison: (a) cranium, (b) mandible, (c) cervical vertebrae, (d) thoracic vertebrae, (e) lumbar vertebrae, (f) sacrum, (g) caudal vertebrae, (h) ribs, (i) sternum, (j) scapula, (k) humerus, (l) radio-ulna, (m) metacarpal, (n) phalanges, (o) pelvis, (p) femur, (q) patella, (r) tibia, (s) calcaneus, (t) astralagus, and (u) metatarsal.

Bone Tool Manufacture

Relatively fresh animal bone can be modified by a variety of techniques, including breaking, grooving, sawing, drilling, and grinding. The methods employed depend on the form and size of the bone and the type of tool desired.

Bone Breaking. Perhaps the simplest and most expedient means of modifying bone is by breaking the bone on an anvil with a large hammerstone. This technique was commonly employed in extracting the nutritious marrow from the bone cavity. Fresh bone is a hard, slightly brittle substance which can be split, broken, and splintered due to its fracture properties. Long bones of large animals can be cracked and broken into sharp splinters suitable for immediate use as picks or scrapers or for further modification into awls and spatulate tools. This technique of breaking bone is relatively haphazard but when coupled with other methods such as grooving or sawing, can be used to shape more sophisticated tools.

Breaking a long bone with a hammerstone and anvil.

Grooving and Splitting. For some delicate bone tools, it is necessary to preform the implement prior to its removal from the parent bone. Sharp pointed gravers and chisel-ended burins were used to scrape deep grooves into bone sections corresponding to the outline of the intended tool. Grooving bone with a modified flake tool can be slow but soaking the bone in water for a few days can speed up the process. Soaking will temporarily soften the bone, making cutting and scraping faster, and once the bone is dry again it will return to its hard, resilient state. In making things like bone awls or needles, grooves outlining the intended tool's form are sawed through the hard outer bone to the spongy cancellous bone. The piece can then be broken free with relative ease.

A graver (left) and its use in grooving bone.

Sawing, Drilling, and Grinding. Bone can be sawed into sections with a slightly serrated bifacial knife or flake tool. After the saw cuts have been made to a sufficient depth the bone can easily be broken by hand. Drills, either hand-held or attached to shafts, may be used to bore holes through bone for making such tools as arrow-shaft wrenches. To widen the holes, hand-held reamers are useful. The small eyes of sewing and matting needles can be made by a sawing or twisting motion with a graver tip. Polishing, final shaping, and sharpening were done against a sandstone abrader. Some tools, like deer phalanx fishhooks, are made almost totally by grinding.

Bone Tool Types

Since bone is not a universally well preserved material, we know little about the bone tool technologies of the cultures prior to the Late Prehistoric period. After A.D. 1000, however, bone tools are well known from the various cultures of Iowa. The Mill Creek culture of northwest Iowa (ca. A.D. 900 to 1400) exhibits a particularly rich assemblage of bone artifacts. Bone tools may be categorized according to their supposed functions, and some of these categories are described below.

Hoes. Late Prehistoric agricultural groups of the Midwest and Plains commonly made hoe blades from the scapulae of bison and elk. These tools are triangular-shaped and require only a few modifications for use. The acromion process, a long spine that runs the length of the bone, may be easily broken off after a few deep saw cuts have been made. Portions

of the anterior border may be broken away to give the blade a more symmetrical appearance. After the broad vertebral border has been beveled and ground sharp, the hoe blade is ready for mounting in a split and notched wooden handle.

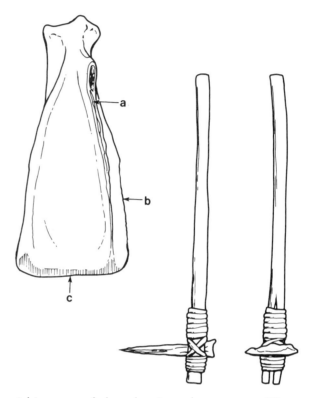

A bison scapula hoe showing subsequent modification and method of hafting: (a) removed acromion process, (b) trimmed anterior border, (c) sharpened vertebral border.

Knives. The so-called squash knives were also made from the scapulae of large mammals. These tools were made by selecting a portion of the broken shoulder blade and grinding the thin interior bone edge sharp. Such tools would have served well in slicing soft, vegetative materials.

Scoops. Scoops were made from the horn core and accompanying portion of the frontal bone of bison. These tools were probably made by breaking off the desired piece of the skull and grinding the exposed edge sharp. Horn scoops were probably used as a hand-held digging tool.

Fleshers. Saw-tooth-edged fleshing tools were commonly made from the long bones of large animals, particularly the metatarsals of bison and elk. By breaking the distal end off at an angle and then sharpening and serrating the exposed edge these tools were made. Such tools were used to strip the fatty tissues from the inner surfaces of fresh animal hides .

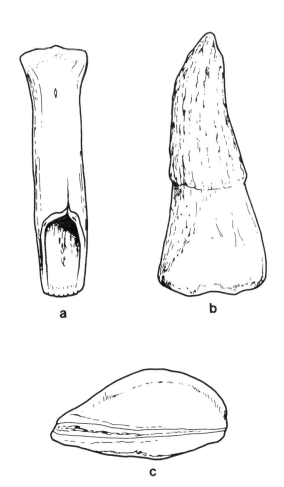

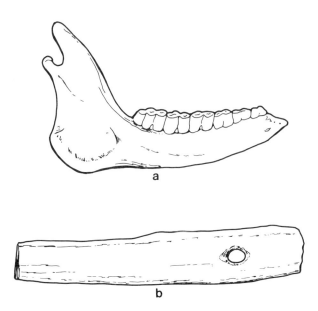

(a) Deer mandible sickle showing worn diastima (arrow), (b) arrow shaft wrench made of bison rib.

(a) Serrated flesher made from a bison metatarsal, (b) scoop made from the horn and frontal bone of a bison skull, (c) "squash knife" made from a section of bison scapula.

Hide Grainers. Tools for scraping and smoothing the inner surfaces of hides were made from the rounded heads of the femora and humeri of large animals. These tools were made by breaking off the proximal ends of a femur or humerus of a bison or comparable animal, and the rough cancellous interior bone exposed was used to abrade hide surfaces.

Sickles. Deer mandibles were used in an unmodified state for threshing grassy plants. The anterior diastema is frequently worked away and polished smooth.

Arrow-Shaft Wrenches. The ribs of bison and elk as well as the long bones of deer were sometimes drilled with holes for use in straightening arrow shafts. These tools were used as wrenches in removing the warps from heated arrow shafts.

Fishhooks. Fishhooks were made by two methods each corresponding to the raw material involved. The proximal phalanges of deer were first cut and split lengthwise, then the exterior surface of the bone was removed by grinding, thus leaving only the hook-shaped ridge of bone inside. Larger fishhooks were made from oval-shaped blanks of split rib by grooving and grinding.

Awls. Awls, used as leather punches in sewing hides, were made from a variety of bones. The ulnae of deer could be cut and removed from the radius and then ground and polished to form a sharp tip. Random as well as preformed splinters of rib and long bone were also ground into awls. Hollow bird bones were sometimes broken and split to form awls as well.

Quill Flatteners. So-called quill flatteners are spatulate-ended tools made from long splinters of mammal bone. The rounded and flattened ends of these

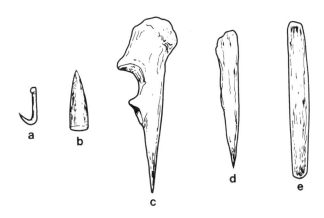

(a) Deer phalanx fishhook, (b) antler tip arrowpoint, (c) deer ulna awl, (d) splinter awl, (e) quill flatterner.

tools have long been thought to have been used in the flattening of porcupine quills for use as decoration, but they may also have been used as pressure flakers in flint knapping.

Antler Artifacts. Like bone, antler is tough and resilient, but unlike bone, antler is relatively solid and varies greatly in form from individual to individual deer. Antlers are grown by the male of the deer species and are shed each year in the winter. Antlers were perhaps most important to prehistoric groups for use as flint knapping tools, being used in both percussion and pressure flaking. Soft hammer batons for controlled percussion flaking were made from the basal portions of antlers by cutting them to length and grinding off the rough burr at the base. Antler tips were often cut to lengths of 3 to 10 inches and were used as pressure flakers. Antler tips were also sometimes cut and drilled to make conical arrowpoints.

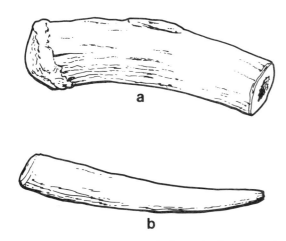

(a) Soft hammer baton made from the basal section of a white-tail deer antler, (b) antler tine pressure flaker

*From a manual prepared for a workshop held at the 33rd Annual Meeting of the Iowa Archeological Society, April 1983.

Illustration Credits

Cover, original illustration by Will Thomson.

Page 2, from *The Grant Oneota Village* by Marshall McKusick. Copyright © 1973 Office of the State Archaeologist, Iowa.

Page 3, from *Iowa Projectile Points* by Toby Morrow. Copyright © 1984 Office of the State Archaeologist, Iowa.

Page 5, illustration by Toby Morrow in Iowa Archeological Society *Newsletter*, No. 103, 1982. Reprinted with permission of the Iowa Archeological Society.

Page 7, from *Pre-Columbian Shell Engravings from the Craig Mound at Spiro, Oklahoma.* by Philip Phillips and James A. Brown, Vol. II, p. xv, Peabody Museum Press, Peabody Museum of Archaeology and Ethnology, Harvard University, Cambridge, Massachusetts. Copyright © 1978 President and Fellows of Harvard College. Reprinted with permission of the publisher.

Page 10 right, from *Agriculture of the Hidatsa Indians: An Indian Interpretation* by Gilbert Livingstone Wilson, 1912, University of Minnesota, Minneapolis.

Page 10 left, from *The Central Plains Tradition: Internal Development and External Relationships* edited by Donald J. Blakeslee. Copyright © 1978 Office of the State Archaeologist, Iowa.

Page 14, recomposed from original drawing by Robert A. and Lynn M. Alex in *The Archeology of Beaver Creek Shelter (39CU779): A Preliminary Statement* by Lynn Marie Alex, 1991, National Park Service, Denver.

Page 17 left, from *Educational Series 3: Woodland* by Lynn M. Alex, 1976, Office of the State Archaeologist, Iowa City.

Page 17 right, from *Mill Creek Ceramics: The Complex from the Brewster Site* by Duane C. Anderson. Copyright © 1981 Office of the State Archaeologist, Iowa.

Page 19 upper, from *Silver Creek Woodland Sites, Southwestern Wisconsin* by William M. Hurley, 1974, Office of the State Archaeologist, Iowa City.

Page 19 lower, composite of original illustration by Eduardo Vega and illustration from *Educational Series 3: Woodland* by Lynn M. Alex, 1976, Office of the State Archaeologist, Iowa City.

Page 23, original illustration by Will Thomson.

Page 25, original illustration by Will Thomson.

Page 27 left, from *Fish, Amphibian and Reptile Remains from Archaeological Sites. Part 1. Southeastern and Southwestern United States* by Stanley J. Olsen, Peabody Museum Papers, Vol. 56, No. 2, p. 199, Peabody Museum, Cambridge, Massachusetts. Copyright © 1968 President and Fellows of Harvard College. Reprinted with permission of the publisher.

Page 27 right, from *Educational Series 2: Archaic* by Lynn M. Alex, 1976, Office of the State Archaeologist, Iowa City.

Page 29, illustration by Wayne Pushetonequa in Iowa Archeological Society *Newsletter*, No. 97, 1980. Reprinted with permission of the artist and the Iowa Archeological Society.

Page 35, illustration by Charles Pushetonequa in Iowa Archeologiacal Society *Newsletter*, No. 78, 1975. Reprinted with permission of Wayne Pushetonequa and the Iowa Archeological Society.

Pages 51–54, adapted from original illustrations by Toby Morrow.

THE IOWA ARCHEOLOGICAL SOCIETY

The Iowa Archeological Society was established in 1951 by Iowans interested in *preserving* and *studying* Iowa's prehistoric and early historic heritage. Its aims are to gather, record, publish and interpret archaeological information in cooperation with career archeologists in the region.

The society is a non-profit scientific society organized under corporate Iowa and federal laws.

WHO MAY JOIN THE SOCIETY?

Any person interested in furthering the goals of the society is invited to join; no previous knowledge or training is necessary.

SOCIETY ACTIVITIES

The Iowa Archeological Society meets annually in the spring and frequently in the fall at various places around the state. The meetings provide an opportunity for exchange of information through workshops, site reports and special lectures for individuals to learn about Iowa's rich and interesting past.

Members may participate in field trips and supervised excavations conducted within the state.

The Iowa Archeological Society has local chapters which also hold meetings and field trips. They are located throughout the state.

WHAT DOES THE SOCIETY OFFER MEMBERS?

All memberships provide opportunities for self-education in Iowa archeology. Two official publications are received by all members—the *Journal of the Iowa Archeological Society*, published annually, and the quarterly *Newsletter*. The *Journal* carries reports of scientific investigations conducted in Iowa, and the *Newsletter* provides the membership a medium for publication of short articles and an opportunity to keep abreast of archeological activities in Iowa.

Illustrated by Mesquakie artist Charles Push-e-to-ne qua.

I wish to become a member of the Iowa Archeological Society.

Name_____

Address _____

City, State _____Zip_____

Please indicate type of membership desired:

Voting Members
_____ Active $15.00
_____ Sustaining $25.00
_____ Household $18.00

Non-Voting Members
_____ Student (under 18) $7.00
_____ Institution $20.00

Make check payable to Iowa Archeological Society
Mail to: Deb Baker, Treasurer, Iowa Archeological Society,
616 7th Avenue, Coralville, Iowa 52241